THEATER

Andrea Gronemeyer

BARRON'S

792.09
G876t

Cover photos from top to bottom and left to right: Josef Kainz as Hamlet / Agamemnon, "Théâtre du Soleil," 1991 / Samuel Beckett / Ludwig Devrient as King Lear, Austrian National Library, Vienna / Ellen Terry as Lady Macbeth, 1887, British Museum, London / Mlle. Dumesnile as Phaedra, François Folliot, Paris / First folio edition of the complete works of Shakespeare, 1623, Royal Shakespeare Theatre, Stratford-upon-Avon / Scene from *Hamlet*, colored print, 19th century, Biblioteca Civica, Turin / Model of a Shakespearean stage, British Travel Association / "New Demons" dance company, 1988, © Bernd Uhlig, Köln / Greek actor with mask, vase painting / Vienna Burgtheater, colored print, 19th century / Aragoto actor / Otto Reigbert, stage design for Bertolt Brecht's *Drums in the Night*, German Museum, Munich / Scene from Ariane Mnouchkine's production of Shakespeare's *Henry IV*, Tita Gaehme, Köln
Back cover from top to bottom: Ulrich Wildgruber as Sophocles' Oedipus the King, Köln / Peter Lühr as Merlin in *Merlin or The Deserted Land*, 1982 / Punch and Judy theater: Kasper, the Devil and the Crocodile
Frontispiece: Pieter Breughel the Younger, *Boerenkermes*, after a painting by Pieter Balten, Fitzwilliam Museum, Cambridge, Massachusetts (see p. 42)

American text version by: Editorial Office Sulzer-Reichel, Rösrath, Germany
Translated by: Sally Schreiber, Friedrichshafen, Germany
Edited by: Bessie Blum, Cambridge, Mass.

First edition for the United States and Canada
published by Barron's Educational Series, Inc., 1996.

First published in the Federal Republic of Germany in 1995 by
DuMont Buchverlag GmbH und Co. Kommanditgesellschaft,
Köln, Federal Republic of Germany.

Text copyright © 1995 DuMont Buchverlag GmbH und Co. Kommanditgesellschaft,
Köln, Federal Republic of Germany.

Copyright © 1996 U.S. language translation, Barron's Educational Series, Inc.

All inquiries should be addressed to:
Barron's Educational Series, Inc.
250 Wireless Boulevard
Hauppauge, New York 11788

Library of Congress Catalog Card No. 96-83722

ISBN 0-8120-9774-2

Printed in Italy by Editoriale Libraria

Contents

Preface 7

From Prehistory to Ancient Greece and Rome 8
- Primitive theater 8
- Theater and civilization 10
- Theater for the polity 13
- Bread and circuses 18

Theater of the Far East 22
- The Indian Nātya'sāstra:
  An early handbook of the dramatic arts 23
- Indonesian shadow theater 26
- The Beijing Opera 27
- The Japanese Nō play—A voyage into the past 30

The Middle Ages 34
- The culture of Christendom 34
- The subculture of the Middle Ages: Wandering players 36
- Religious drama 38
- Secular drama 42
- *Theater Spaces* 44

Transition to Modernity 50
- Entry into a new world 50
- From pastoral drama to opera 55
- Theater of the schools 58

The Golden Age of Theater 60
- "All the world's a stage" 60
- Theater as spectacle 64
- England: Shakespeare and the age of Elizabeth 69
- Spain's great world theater 78
- France: Classical tragedy, comedy of character 82
- *The Actress* 88

Bourgeois Theater 94
- The age of Enlightenment 94
- Moving into the 18th century 100
- The curtain rises on the German theater 102
- From "Sturm und Drang" to Weimarer classic 105

Theater and Reality 110
- The romantic reaction 110
- Innovation in Meiningen 115
- The perfect illusion: Naturalism 117
- The Russians are coming 123
- *Film—The Great Competitor* 128

Art and Politics 132
- Modern world utopias 133
- In the right light 136
- Political theater 140
- *Children's Theater* 150

Theater Today 154
- The economics of theater 156
- "There's no business like show business" 158
- International independent theater 165
- The opportunity of the theater 169

Glossary 172
A brief overview of theater history 174
Theater collections 177
Bibliography 179
Subject index 182
Index of names 186
Picture credits 192

Preface

Anyone who wonders why theater, despite common charges to the contrary, continues to claim its place in the cultural landscape, may find an answer in this Crash Course on Theater. "Crash Course" means that this book attempts to present a brief but vivid picture of the past history and present state of the theater and of the many different forms of theatrical art found around the world. The book covers Far Eastern theatrical spectacles and Western dramatics; the vicissitudes of a theater under religious ban and state censorship; the brilliance of court theater and the misery of itinerant comedians; the longings of the bourgeoisie for a free artistic existence, and the revolutionary drive to overcome the boundaries between life and art.

To theater enthusiasts on both sides of the footlights, this book offers something about the development of the stage and costumes, acting technique and direction, show business and the avant garde, scandals, leading men and leading ladies, and of course dramatists.

Admittedly, such a book is no substitute for a guide to dramatic literature, since dramatic literature per se is not in the limelight of such a "crash course," but rather theater as a total work of art, comprised of acting, text, music, setting, and playing area. Nor is this survey a compendium of facts; rather, without claiming to be exhaustive, it is designed to convey an overview of the critical personalities and events that have brought about aesthetic changes and theatrical progress in a given era.

A supplementary glossary, a summary of prominent theater archives and museums, and suggestions for further reading show the reader the way to a deeper understanding of the world of theater.

The best "crash course," however, is to be found in the theater itself. No book can replace the fascination of the meeting between actor and audience, or capture the evanescent magic of the most transitory of all art forms. This little book will have fulfilled its real purpose if it lures the reader into the theater.

Andrea Gronemeyer

Prehistory – 400 A.D.

15,000–9000 B.C. Late Stone Age cave paintings: Altamira (Spain), Lascaux and Trois Frères (France)

ca. 7000 B.C. Agriculture and stock breeding

ca. 3000–332 B.C. Egyptian kingdoms

1200–1000 B.C. Greek migrations

776 B.C. First evidence of Olympic Games

750–550 B.C. Colonization and founding of Greek city-states

ca. 750 B.C. Foundation of Rome; Homer: *The Iliad* and *The Odyssey*

509 B.C. Cleisthenes establishes democracy in Greece

484–425 B.C. Herodotus

470–27 B.C. Republic of Rome

449 B.C. End of the Persian wars

447 B.C. Reconstruction of the Acropolis

404 B.C. Reintroduction of oligarchy in Greece

399 B.C. Death of Socrates

387 B.C. Plato's Academy

335 B.C. Aristotle, *Poetics*

326 B.C. and later Hellenism: Greek culture dominates from Asia Minor to the Indus

266 B.C. Rome controls the Mediterranean; the *Imperium Romanum* is established

27 B.C.–460 A.D. The Roman Empire

64 A.D. Burning of Rome instigates the persecution of the Christians under Nero

325 A.D. Emperor Constantine: Christianity is declared the state religion

What do we think about when we think about "theater"? Today, we naturally think of actors and actresses performing a drama on stage before an audience. The art of theater in this sense has in fact existed for more than 2,500 years, but the search for the historical beginnings of theater—of mimetic action—will carry us all the way back to the Stone Age. And if we were to ask an anthropologist about the geographical origin of theater, he or she is likely to explain that theatrical activity as a form of social interchange can be found in almost every culture in the world.

Thus, we may call theater a universal human language, more primary than the cult rituals themselves, even though these rituals are generally accepted to be the source of theater. Rather, theater springs from the deep human instinct to imitate, to communicate with and alter the perceived universe. Anyone who observes growing children can see how they learn to deal with their world through fantasy play and mimicry. The child imitates reality and at the same time imposes her own vision on reality. The playing of children and the theatrical play of actors in a drama both reveal the human impulse to deny the absoluteness of reality, but instead to alter reality "magically" in play, and through play to transform reality.

Primitive theater

The cave paintings of the Stone Age provide us with knowledge of the very earliest forms of theater. The Ice Age hunter who draped himself in the pelt of

The Magician, from the Trois Frères cave in the French Pyrenees, is one of many representations of humans costumed as animals. Crafted between 30,000 B.C. and 13,000 B.C., the drawing is among the earliest evidences of theatrical role playing.

Cave paintings, such as this depiction of dancing hunters in leopard-skin wraps (Catal Hüyük, Turkey), indicate the use of masks, costumes, props, and musical instruments.

Prehistory – 400 A.D.

a predator in order to assume its animal powers or who donned the mask of his victim in the hope of approaching his prey as silently as possible— our ancient hunter, who may even have lacked the ability to speak, acted out around his campfire the adventure of the hunt.

Only later did mankind begin to act out similar plays before the hunt itself. Thus arose the ceremonial dances with the intention of magically influencing the outcome of the hunt.

Even today the rituals of so-called primitive tribes are meant to guarantee fertility, successful hunting, or a good harvest. The course of nature, the joy of life, as well as community events are celebrated "theatrically." The presence of comic elements and the treatment of mundane life in such ceremonies prove that the human race has long appreciated the sheer entertainment value of

One of the earliest human dramas is the struggle against an animal. For the Bambuti pygmies of the Ituri Valley, such a drama provides daily entertainment: "A chimpanzee dance demands particular power of expression on the part of the dancers. Performed only by men and boys, the troupe moves in staggering dance steps through the entire camp, grimacing as they go. The oldest dancer, armed with bow and arrow, represents a hunter who has drawn aside from the chimpanzee hunt, hidden behind a bush or tree to spy on the herd, and drawn his bow against them. The cunning chimpanzees, however, had already sighted him and confront him with gestures of both anger and fear. The arrow whirs; the herd dodges and ducks out of the way, grinning and howling. The play is repeated several times to the accompaniment of threatening drumrolls." (O. Eberle)

Prehistory – 400 A.D.

An African war dance. A primary source of theater is dance. As a manifestation of the need to give bodily expression to spiritual experiences, dance is fundamental to religious ceremonies throughout the world.

this theatrical playing. The need of human beings to transform themselves and their world through mime suggests that theater lies at the source of human art and may well constitute the spring of all other arts.

Balinese children's frog dance.

The many surviving pictures of dancers, musicians, and female acrobats testify to the role of theatrical play among the worldly pleasures of the pharaohs' courts.

Theater and civilization

With the emergence of the first civilizations around 4000 B.C., theater also entered a new era.

In the fertile river basins between the Tigris and the Euphrates, and along the Nile, the Indus, and the Hwangho, the sharing of the great agricultural labors led to the growth of larger communities, which in turn freed a portion of the population from the necessity of producing its own food. The excess time gained by the community allowed for the development of trade, handcrafts and metalwork, writing and art.

This new, differentiated society also developed a new social order, based on a complex state administration and governed by priest-kings who

ruled as representatives of the deity. One might say that the heavens themselves bowed to this new impulse toward clarity and order: the prehistoric chaos of demonic animals was humanized into a community of gods.

Egyptian artists preferred to depict the myths themselves rather than the dramatizations staged during religious festivals. We may never know whether the gods' battleship in the *Osiris Mystery Cycle* actually sailed over the Nile or whether it was carried, as in this drawing of priests carrying the bark of the god Amun.

With the development of mythology, mankind freed itself from the stifling fear of demons and began the task of interpreting the creation and meaning of the world. This intellectual and spiritual development is evident in the body of art and monumental architecture of the ancient world. With gigantic temples as a stage, theater evolved from a primitive ritual to a great theatrical festival. Often lasting several days, performances arose from the need to present, and to spread, the fundamental tenets of the new state religions.

The oldest religious mystery plays

During the Egyptian Middle Kingdom (2000–1500 B.C.), the city of Abydos became the showplace of the annual mystery plays that treated the suffering, death, and resurrection of the god Osiris. Thanks to notes inscribed on a clay tablet by a member of the audience, the court official I-Cher-Nofret, we know of some of the acts in this theatrical procession.

Acrobatic dancers such as this, which dates from the 19th dynasty of the New Kingdom, took part not only in the worldy entertainment of the court, but also in religious plays.

The performance began with the departure of the god in a holy bark. Accompanied by the war god Wep-Wapnet, Osiris fought his enemies in a bloody battle. Of the murder of Osiris and his dismemberment by his brother Seth, we have no exact knowledge because this scene was one of the secret rituals of the play. The next scene, however, is a procession in which the bark containing an image of Osiris is brought

The *Ramses Papyrus* (ca. 1850 B.C.) is believed to be the oldest surviving written drama. It depicts an Osiris ritual that might have been part of a coronation ceremony. The illustrated scenes at the bottom of every block of text suggest that the papyrus describes not only the myth but its presentation within the framework of a religious ceremony.

The legend of the death of the god Osiris, resurrected after he was killed by his brother Seth and avenged by his posthumous son Horus, stems from a fertility myth. The Egyptians experienced the annual flooding of their desiccated fields, and humanized it in the myth of Osiris who drowned in water and returned again to life. Only later was the idea of a life after death applied to human beings.

to his grave. After the burial, the struggle breaks out again, but Horus, the son of Osiris, triumphs as avenger. The final mystery, enacted in the secret inner regions of the temple, was also hidden from the public—and hence also from us. The plays were performed by priests and privileged members of the laity. From the description of a similar ceremony by the Greek historian Herodotus describing how the theatrical battles often resulted in the drawing of real blood, we may surmise how strongly the

Little has survived from the religious festival dramas enacted before the gigantic temple buildings of the Americas. However, numerous drawings of musicians, acrobats, and masked jugglers, such as this Mayan vase painting, show a startling resemblance to similar depictions from the high cultures of the Old World.

interplay of dramatic passions moved some of the participating players.

Theater for the polity

Theater, teatro, théâtre, teater, teatr—our modern words for the performing arts derive from the Greek term for "viewing place," *theatron*. This ancient theatron is in fact the cradle of Western dramatic art. The establishment of a place for the audience was a decisive development in the history of the theater. The ritual community dramas that had centered on fertility and the cult of death were now drawn into the service of a new societal form, democracy; they were transformed into a political convocation and given a worldly orientation. The theatrical action no longer sought to bridge the gap between the participants and the magically powerful gods, but played to the now wholly passive audience of the Greek city-state.

Classical theater, thus, arose from the desire to instill a civic identity in the Attic citizens, an identity that would bind them to the state community. The importance of theater in the life of the city-state is clear from the introduction in the late 4th century B.C. of a theater allowance paid out to the apparently ever less highly motivated citizenry—after all, attendance at the festival was a civic duty—for the work days lost during the theater holidays.

The Great Dionysian Festival

During the 6th century B.C., the differences between the ruling nobles and the commoners drawn from the countryside to defend the city-state came to a head. Supported by the peasant farmers, Peisistratus set up a tyrannical autocracy in Athens, which was transformed by Cleisthenes in 509 B.C. into the first democracy.

Prehistory – 400 A.D.

Protagoras
(ca. 485–410 B.C.)
"Man is the measure of all things."

Socrates
(ca. 470–399 B.C.)
"The wise man is the man who knows he does not know. A right understanding leads to right behavior."

Plato
(428/27–348/47 B.C.)
"The perceived world is only a distorted shadow of the world of abstract ideas—reason, not perception, leads to truth."

Aristotle
(384–322 B.C.)
"Abstract truth is derived not from reason, but from the sum of all sensory perceptions. Art imitates reality."

Epicurus
(341–270 B.C.)
"Pleasure is the beginning and end of a happy life."

Players preparing for a performance.

It was Peisistratus who first brought together the Dionysian cult plays, especially loved by the peasants and workers, into a state festival, the Great Dionysian Festival. The god of fertility and wine thus advanced to become the protector of the city and, after the introduction of the tragedy contests (*agon*), the patron of the theater. The citizens of the polity gathered in the theatron before the performance to discuss pressing questions of politics and law. In the agon of the Great Dionysian Contest, tragedians competed against each other in presenting a tetralogy (series of four plays) of three tragedies presented on three successive days, followed by a *satyr* play. The poets also functioned as directors, choreographers, and characters in their own original productions, and each was supported by a *choregen*, a patron who took on the honorable role of assembling a chorus of citizens and feeding them during the rehearsals.

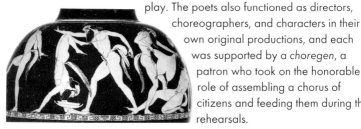

Lecherous satyrs are easily recognized by their phalluses, horsetails, and ears. They belonged originally to the train of Dionysus, whom they honored with orgiastic dances.

Drama and the types of stages

Already in the 6th century B.C., the presentation of the dramas shifted from the *agora*, the assembly place of the *city-state*, to the Dionysian theater, erected specifically for this purpose. The huge *theatron* was nestled into the southern slope

Types of Stages

of the Acropolis and almost completely enclosed the circular orchestra, where the chorus in the early days of tragedy danced and played an active role in the plot. The view of the orchestra was—as is appropriate in a democracy—almost equally good from any position.

According to the chronicle of 534 B.C., the first winner of a tragedy contest was the legendary Thespis. It was supposedly Thespis who expanded the song of the chorus (*dithyrambos*) into a dramatic dialogue by creating a character who "answered" the chorus. As counter to this protagonist, Aeschylus developed a second character (*deuteragonist*), and Sophocles finally added a third (*tritagonist*).

In the *skene*, the small hut that closed off the far end of the orchestra, the players changed their costumes and masks as needed for their various roles. Not until the 3rd century B.C. was the skene expanded to include an overhanging roof (*proskenion*) and machinery to raise and lower the *deus ex machina*—the god who conventionally appeared suddenly and solved the situation.

As the chorus was pushed ever further into the background, the action also moved from the orchestra to the proskenion.

Tragedy

We know the names of 46 tragic poets and of more than 600 of their plays, but only a few complete dramas have survived. The themes of the plays invariably derive from Greek mythology, but by the time of the introduction of democracy, these fables about the

The actor contemplating his mask is a favorite theme of the ancient amphora paintings of the 5th century B.C.

Stone "theater tickets."

The chorus often appeared in satyr costumes, as on this amphora from 425 B.C. The three zither players are participating in a dithyrambos contest in honor of Dionysus (right).

15

Classical tragedy required expressively sculptured masks, typically with wide-opened eyes and mouth. In the "dreadful masks" of Aeschylus, the expression of suffering or fear was set.

The magnificent gown with long train, 8-inch platform shoes, and the oversized mask with wig prevailed in Hellenistic theater. For tragedy, flat shoes and floor-length robes were used to allow swift movement.

Aeschylus (525/24–456/55 B.C.) stands as the father of artistic tragedy. Of his 90 works, with which he won the tragedy contest 13 times, 7 plays survive: *The Persians, Seven against Thebes, The Hiketiden, The Oresteia* (including *Agamemnon, The Choephori,* and *The Eumenides*), and *Prometheus Bound* (though recent scholarship has suggested that this last was in fact written after Aeschylus's death).

power of the gods and the will of man served merely as an occasion to engage the public in current issues and politics. Man as an object of fate, a central concept in the old myths, was challenged and gave way to an increasing emphasis on the free will of human beings and their ability to determine their own fates. The works of Aeschylus, whose trilogy, the *Oresteia*, brought him fame in his own day, helped to consolidate the city-state by portraying the transition from a mythological understanding of life to a community based on law. Aeschylus's pupil Sophocles devoted himself to exploring the question of what it means to be human. His *Oedipus Rex*, the first mystery story in world literature, is an example of a new concentration on the tragic conflict within the individual, and still impresses audiences today with its tightly wrought dramaturgy. Influenced by the worldly orientation of the Sophists, Euripides, Sophocles' chief rival, denied the power of the gods altogether. In *Electra* and *The Trojan Women*, Euripides' depiction of characters caught in an extremely complex social and political network defines a new understanding of human nature.

Tragedy as an art form survived the collapse of the polis at the end of the 5th century. But spectacular scenography and the virtuosity of the actors were forcing the achievement of the dramatic poets into the shadows. This devaluation is

Comedy

Aristotle's target in his *Poetics*: for him, Sophocles provides the ideal model of the art of tragedy. Staging and mere dramatic virtuosity—"spectacle"—counted as nothing for Aristotle; on the contrary, the art of tragedy consisted in the ability to arouse fear (*phobos*) and pity (*eleas*) in the audience in order to effect a cleansing (*katharsis*) of these emotions. For Aristotle, this serious philosophical intention makes tragedy supreme among the poetic arts.

"Let me, O Athenians, tell you the truth for once ..."

The term "comedy" originally referred to a riotous masked dancing procession. Comedy successfully adopted the folk customs of the phallic and Dionysian cults and became the favorite genre of the Hellenistic period. Comedy, which always provided the harmlessly cheerful conclusion to a tragic tetralogy, distinguished itself from similarly pleasure-happy satyr plays through its satire. Heroes from the myths were ridiculed just as mercilessly as contemporary heroes, poets, and philosophers.

When Athens lost its hegemony in the Attic Sea League, Aristophanes, the greatest of the ancient comic poets, could scarcely conceal his criticism of democracy, its champion Pericles, and his ideological precursors, the Sophists. Thus, even the so-called Old Comedy of the Greek theater remained a form of political discussion.

With the end of the democracy, Middle Comedy turned away from political themes and aimed its ridicule at everyday figures such as braggarts and ill-tempered mothers-in-law. Menander, an exponent of the New Comedy, composed over 100 comedies in which he refined the traditional comic figures into more developed characters and eliminated the chorus as well as all political commentary.

Sophocles (497/96 – 407 B.C.), who won the dramatic contest 18 times, was honored as a minion of the gods. Within his own lifetime, his books were published and read in schools. Only 7 of his 123 dramas survive: *Ajax, Antigone, Trachiniae (The Women of Trachis), Oedipus Tyrannus, Electra, Philoctetes,* and *Oedipus at Colonus.*

Euripides (ca. 484 – 406 B.C.) achieved success only after his death—he won only five of the Great Dionysian Contests. Of his 92 plays, 17 remain, among them: *Alcestis, Media, Iphigenia in Taurus, Electra, The Trojan Women,* and *The Bacchae.*

Aristophanes (450/45 – ca. 388 B.C.), the chief representative of Old Greek Comedy, attacked the war-mongering of his contemporaries, as well as satirized a variety of contemporary social ills. In his most popular play, *Lysistrata,* the women of Athens and Sparta hold a sex strike to force the men to end the war.

The phallic origin in comedy can be seen in the glaring emphasis of the costumes on the genitals.

The traces of a nonliterary theater tradition reach back into the 6th century B.C. *Mimus* and *Phlyaken* farces were originally improvised forms of comic popular theater, which typically used grotesque masks and exaggerated stomachs.

Thievery was an extremely popular theme in Attic comedy. This vase depicts a miser being dragged out of his house by two robbers.

Bread and circuses

The triumph of Roman culture was the result of a massive war of conquest, but the war booty did not consist of material goods alone: in the 3rd century B.C., Rome effected the wholesale importation of Hellenic culture into its civilization. Rome took over the Olympian gods and the inspiration of Greek architecture, art, and philosophy. Greek slaves were highly desirable teachers for Roman students. The destruction of Carthage in the First Punic War raised Rome to a great power in 240 B.C.; in the same year, the Roman Senate ordered the introduction of theater presentations as a part of the *ludi Romani*, the Roman city festival. The Greek freedman Livius Andronicus was commissioned to compose the first Latin tragedy.

As it had been in Greece, theater in Rome was at first considered akin to a state institution—with one important difference: the theater of the polis had functioned as a forum for political discussion, where Roman theater served chiefly as a demon-

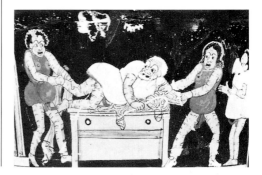

Bread and Circuses

2nd-century Roman mosaics of tragic and comic masks.

stration of state power. Buying the favor of the people with "bread and circuses" proved highly effective in diverting their attention from internal political conflicts. Theatrical entertainment competed for the attention of the masses against such popular spectacles as gladiator contests, animal baiting, and public executions.

Seneca (4 B.C.–65 A.D.) based his dramas on Greek tragedy. With similes from mythology, he portrayed the unscrupulous lust for power and monstrous violence of imperial Rome.

The triumph of entertainment

Under these circumstances, it is no wonder that Roman tragedy did not succeed as well as comedy, and with the exception of the chamber dramas of Seneca, none has survived. From the coarse popularistic plays of Plautus—which were actually reworkings of Greek New Comedy—we have inherited 20 slave farces, mythological travesties, and comedies of mistaken identity. Plautus depended on spectacular jests and a fast tempo, for which he occasionally even sacrificed plot development. Terence, who showed rather more literary ambition, apparently renounced vulgar humor in favor of comedy of character and finished dramatic technique in his six surviving plays.

With the growth of the Roman Empire in the 1st century B.C., folk theater supplanted comedy as the most popular theatrical form. In the *pantomimus*, a singer or simply a chorus with

A scene from the comedy *Cistellaria* by Plautus (ca. 254–184 B.C.). The masked old woman complains to her hostesses about the quality of the wine.

19

An ancient painting from a southern Italian amphora showing a post-Euripides production of *Medea*.

This painting from the 9th century A.D., based on a 4th-century original, portrays a scene from *Adelphoe* by Terence (186/85 – 159 B.C.).

orchestral accompaniment declaimed a story whose various roles were interpreted by a soloist using masks, dancing, and a highly developed sign language. *Attellane*, written in the ancient Italian language Oscan, was based on improvisation with a set of grotesque masks and four stock characters: the simpleton Maccus, the glutton Dossenus, the braggart Bucco, and the old man Pappus.

Adultery in all its forms was the theme of the Roman *mimus*, which was imported from Greece but performed without masks, and was the first theater event known to have women acting the female roles. This allowed the mime artists to present the sex scenes more naturalistically, and to crown the performance with a striptease. Of course, the later Church patriarchs excoriated this wicked amusement, though the sexual explicitness may have given them ammunition in their attempts to suppress the mime's particularly vociferous ridiculing of the rites of the new Church. In the 4th century A.D., rejection of the theater became part of the baptismal vows; in the 5th century a Sunday visit to the theater invited excommunication.

Roman dancers.

But even the closing of all theaters by the Emperor Justinian I (529 A.D.) could do nothing to prevent theatrical play on the streets and at annual markets—or so the surviving repeated edicts against mime and pantomime would suggest.

Prehistory – 400 A.D.

Glossary

Attellane: comic masked folk theater, originally from Attella, experienced a golden age in Rome, ca. 364–103 B.C.

Chorege: financier of the chorus for a production of a Greek tragedy.

Dithyramb: choreographed choral song, considered the origin of ancient drama.

Greater Dionysia: an Athenian state cult, originally a celebration of the god Dionysus, gave rise to the dithyramb and ultimately to Greek drama.

Mimus: initially, improvised Greek folk theater without masks; after 430 B.C., also written.

Orchestra: place for the choral dances.

Palliata: Roman adaptation of New Greek Comedy, named after the kind of costume used (*pallium* = Greek robe).

Pantomimus: voiceless drama of gestures, accompanied by flutes or orchestra and chorus; its golden age was during the Roman Empire.

Phlyaken farce: Greek and lower Italian folk comedy with grotesque masks and costumes; written forms from ca. 300 B.C.

Proskenion: the fore-stage in front of the dressing area (*skene*).

Poetic: a canon of rules for the composition of poetic literature.

Protagonist: the first, and originally the only, actor of Greek tragedy; later supplemented by a second (*deuteragonist*) and a third (*tritagonist*) player.

Satyr play: comic Greek play based on folk tales; in the Greater Dionysia contests, the satyr was always bound together with three tragedies to make a tetralogy.

Skene: the "dressing" area of the Greek stage.

Togata: an independent Roman comedy played in togas, in contrast to the costumed *palliata*.

ca. 3000 B.C.   Religious temple dances of the Indus cults

ca. 1000 B.C.   *Rigveda*, 5th book of the oldest Sanskrit texts

5th century B.C.   China: Lao-Tse founds Taoism; Buddha teaches in India

200 B.C.–200 A.D.   Creation of the *Nātya'sāstra*

100 A.D.   Invention of paper in China

200–900 A.D.   Development of *Sanskrit* drama in India

7th–8th century A.D.   *Gigaku* and *Bugaku*, masked dance plays from China and Korea, reach Japan

ca. 1000 A.D.   Indian shadow play spreads throughout Asia

627–649 A.D.   China's golden age of culture, Emperor Tsi-tsung; Tang collection of 48,900 poems by 2,000 poets

750 A.D.   World's first theater school in China

1275–92 A.D.   The age of Marco Polo: Europe becomes aware of Oriental culture

13th–14th century A.D.   Moralistic heroic drama and erotic love drama in China

ca. 1478 A.D.   Japan's age of heroic feudalism (*Sengoko*)

19th century A.D.   Creation of the Chinese opera

1858 A.D.   India becomes a British Crown colony

With the collapse of the ancient world, at the time when Western drama was succumbing to a long Dark Age, theater in the Far East was blossoming into a number of different dramatic forms. The highly formalized Sanskrit theater achieved a golden age between the 4th and 8th centuries A.D., and in 750 the Chinese emperor Xuangzong established the world's first theater school in his Pear Garden. In Indonesia the delicate shadow play (*Wayang Kulit*) developed at the turn of the first millenium.

Whereas Western dramatic history is characterized by discontinuity, stylistic change, and inconsistency, the theater of the Far East grew from the fertile soil of tradition and emulation. In the actor dynasties of Japan and China, the secrets of dramatic art and role conceptions are still being passed down from father to son. Thus, the Beijing Opera, the Japanese Nō play, and the Indian dance theater have ripened over the centuries into the high classical forms that they remain today. Not always accessible to the Western theatergoer, they are nonetheless extensions of the roots in ritual common to all dramatic forms.

Barong play, Bali. Whereas theatrical tradition in the West has survived largely in written form, in the Far East literary drama has always been regarded as inferior. Far Eastern theater is a combination of visual and musical arts. Spoken drama developed only under the influence of colonialism.

Multidimensional art

In both the Eastern and the Western hemispheres, ritual dance lies at the very heart of drama. This is particularly true for Indian theater, where the words for drama, "*nātaka/nātya*" are derived from the word for dance, "*nāt.*" Still, in China and Japan, whose cultures were strongly influenced by Indian Buddhism, music, dance, and theatrical performance also constitute an inseparable whole.

Acrobatic monkey-army dancers from the Thai dance theater, *Khon.*

Antiquity – Present

Over the centuries, Far Eastern theater has developed a highly complex and symbolic system of rules for gesture, body movement, masks, and costumes. Indeed, naturalistic representation of reality is unlikely to be of much interest to a theater anchored in religion (such as the Nō plays) or to the theatrically spectacular Kabuki plays or the Beijing Opera. Eastern theater, rather, seeks to reveal the truth behind the appearance of the world. Simple, straightforward plots serve merely as an occasion to present feelings, which are then transferred to the audience. The world is structurally divided into a finally victorious good and a conquered evil, while both the characters and the audience remain aware of the illusionary nature of the performance. In the West, this original nature of theater is preserved in only a few forms, such as the *commedia dell'arte*.

The Indian Nātya'sāstra:
An early handbook of the dramatic arts

According to Indian mythology, dance and drama are a gift of the gods. At a time when the world was given over to sensual pleasure, Indra, king of the gods, asked Brahma to create a new form of diversion. The creator, Brahma, inspired the holy scholar Bharata Muni with the codex of

Dance Theater of Burma. The players strive for the effect of human marionettes: the highly stylized body language derives not from nature, but from art, and is reminiscent of stone temple figures. The pure artificiality symbolizes strength, repose, and beauty.

23

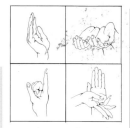

Finger language from Indian dance and drama, upper left to lower right: "good," "I surrender," "this," "the sun."

theatrical art, the Nātya'sāstra, *A Treatise on Theater*. This oldest dramaturgical work in the world in fact delineates a highly developed theatrical culture in India in its early stages of development (200 B.C.–200 A.D.).

The Nātya'sāstra defines not only styles of acting and the poetics of drama, but also everything from the construction and furnishing of a theater to the design of costumes and masks, the timbre of voices and instruments, the socially determined gaits and fixed gestures of the characters, and the relations with courtesans. This handbook distinguishes, for example, among 24 different positions for the fingers, 36 for the eyes, 13 for the head, and 16 for the feet, either suspended in air or on the ground—in addition to plenty of other gestures for eyebrow, nose, neck, chin, and torso.

Indian dance theater

The roots of Indian theater reach back at least 3,000 years to the ritual religious dances performed in and around the temples. A thousand years later, dramatic dialogue appears in the oldest texts of Sanskrit literature, the *Vedas*. The impulse behind the development of ancient Indian drama springs from the humanizing of the gods in the ancient Sanskrit epics, the *Rāmāyana* and the *Mahābhārata*.

Dance and music remained equally important for two more millenia in India, down to the

From the temple dance *Bharata Nātyam*, along with Sanskrit literature and the entertainments of roving jugglers, we get classical Indian theater.

Antiquity – Present

period of classical Sanskrit drama (200–900 A.D.). Unlike the ancient Indian drama, the more romantic Sanskrit theater concerned the amorous adventures of gods and princes and was staged in its own theaters. The roofed stage area was divided by a curtain into a front stage for the performance and a back stage for sound effects, while the audience was seated in the open on three sides of the acting area. There were no stage decorations or props: illusion was created by the pantomime of the players. Both plot and character were governed by the three-tiered *Rasa* theory. In the first phase, the existential feelings of the characters were presented with maximum beauty and charm, in order to touch the hearts of the audience (this constituted the

In the folk theater of Kerala (southern India), exquisite headdresses and costumes, painted masks, as well as passionate dramatic expression have made the classical dance drama *Kathakali* a visual treat since the 15th century.

A miniature depicting a scene from the most famous *Sanskrit* drama, the *Sakuntalā* by Kalidasa.

second phase), and then to bring them into a state of complete bliss, beyond feelings (phase three). Thus, the Rasa theory of Indian dance theater mandated a harmonious ending.

Today, we find countless regional forms of popular theater that evolved from Sanskrit drama in the Middle Ages and moved into the streets—although somewhat faded under the influence of the Moslem invasions. The first permanent theaters were the preserve of the English colonials. National consciousness in the 20th century has led to the development of a

Kathakali is performed only by male dancers who are trained from early childhood in the disciplined repertoire of eye, hand, and foot movements.

new theater that effectively blends the modern with the traditional.

Indonesian shadow theater

Among the many forms of Asian theater, an outstanding and unqiue specialty is the shadow play that spread from southern India throughout Asia more than 1,000 years ago. On the Indonesian islands of Java and Bali, the *wayang* grew to dominate theater. Different forms of shadow theater, such as *wayang golek*, which uses three-dimensional puppets with movable heads and arms, or *wayang klitik*, using flat figures, often made from water-buffalo hide, with one movable arm, began as illustrations to narration, originally drawing tales of gods, heroes, and ritual from Indian epics such as the *Rāmāyana* and the *Mahābhārata*, with a sprinkling of topical and sexual matters added in. During a performance, at least 60, sometimes 100, delicately cut two-dimensional figures are operated by a single puppetmaster, called a *dalang*. A good dalang lends each puppet its own voice and brings each of the artfully painted figures magically to life by manipulating two thin sticks. The obligatory *gamelan* orchestra accompanies the performances which often last from sundown to sunrise. The audience—very few of whom actually have the precise knowledge of the many-layered symbolism necessary to follow a complete performance—is seated according to social rank. Like the body language of Indian dance theater, the construction of the shadow figures follows set rules. Each detail of the complex silhouette has meaning. A thin nose, flat

"The shadow play is the play of life in which our visible deeds are reflected. ... These shadows are the original cause of the existence of natural man, the eternal ideal according to which he was created."
    (Subroto Kusmardjo, Java)

Wayang golek: extremely popular Javanese puppet theater. The three-dimensional, beautifully painted wooden figures are visibly manipulated by the *dalang* before the audience. The repertoire of plays corresponds to that of the *wayang kulit*.

Antiquity – Present

forehead, and slanted eyes connote respectability, while a powerful hero may be recognized through his thick nose, rounded forehead, and round eyes.

Today the shadow play provides more than mere entertainment for its audience: the ancient mystic shadow play has survived all the religious changes of Indonesian history. The play connects the audience with its cultural ancestors through its use of corporeal shadows.

The Beijing Opera

The Beijing Opera is the culmination of 1,000 years of Chinese theatrical art. In its grandiose mixture of styles, the Opera is a compendium of everything that wandering troupes of players during the Ming dynasty found worthwhile on their excursions through the various styles of regional theater—finished pieces, stray melodies, makeup and masks, costumes, patterns of movement, and techniques of stage fighting; there was even a form of "opera" in

Wayang wong: Indonesian dance drama performed by human dancers instead of puppets. With a combination of slow and abrupt movements, while the arms and legs are lifted to a horizontal position, the dancers try to imitate as closely as possible the language of gestures characteristic of the *wayang kulit*. In this variant of the *wayang*, the *dalang* only recites narrative bridges between the players' dialogues.

Wayang topeng: a masked pantomime whose story is narrated by the *dalang*.

27

Wayang klitik: play using flat painted figures with movable leather arms.

Wayang bébér: play without actors. To the commentary of the *dalang*, a cloth scroll with a painted representation of the story is unrolled.

The King of Chu is in fact a villain, as the white background of his mask indicates; however, the black circles around the eyes and the long black beard soften him into an "honorable rogue." The ornamentally curved eyebrows symbolize long life.

northern China of the 18th century, called "clapper opera," based on a complex system of rhythms. Supported by the royal court, this 19th-century stage spectacle became established as a national theater. The well-known texts of the more than 2,000 repertory pieces are drawn from Chinese history and celebrate heroism as the highest fulfillment of earthly existence.

In the Beijing Opera, the Chinese audience enjoys above all the highly individualized interpretations of traditional fables and characters rendered with virtuosity. The Opera creates harmony out of its diverse components of poetry, music, acrobatics, and formal configurations. The falsetto voices, accompanied by drums and

Zhou dynasty (1000–256 B.C.): animal pantomimes and shaman dances; 8th century B.C.: first performances of dance theater in religious festivals; 7th century B.C.: court jugglers and storytellers.

Han dynasty (206 B.C.–220 A.D.): "A Hundred Kinds of Games"—simple presentations; along with sword swallowing, and tightrope walking, actors performed short scenes and farces.

Tang period (618–917 A.D.): first theater school in the world in the Pear Garden of the Emperor Xuangzong; beginning of role stereotyping, the trademark of Chinese theater.

Song period (960–1279 A.D.): growth of trade and crafts; establishment of metropolitan pleasure districts including the clownish bordello theaters.

Yuan dynasty (1280–1368 A.D.): moral heroic dramas (northern school) and erotic love drama (southern school) are productions of the literary theater; most famous is Li Xindao's *Chalk Circle*.

Ming period (1368–1644): roving troupes, 341 local drama forms.

19th century: Beijing Opera spreads throughout China, becoming the national theater.

20th century: spoken drama, in contrast to traditional musical theater, develops through Western influence.

In this painting of the face of the Monkey King, *Sun Wukong*, the nose and the hair around the forehead and mouth are animal characteristics, but the gold around his eyes signifies immortality.

Antiquity – Present

The blue background of this mask from the Beijing Opera expresses this character's fierce courage. The black around the eyes reveals his dignified kindness, while the golden ornament on his forehead signifies his super-natural power. The long white hairs extending from the nose identify the mask as a blue dragon of the heavenly army.

string instruments, bear virtually no resemblance to Western conceptions of operatic arias; rather, the Westerner is fascinated by the daring acrobatics and by the performers' sumptuous costumes and masks.

The symbolism of the highly decorated painted masks is clear only to the initiated. The coloring of a mask establishes clearly whether a character is good (black), evil (white), untrustworthy (green), or simply old (orange). The stage is bordered by ornate tapestries and changes of scene must be spoken or demonstrated. Flags bearing simple symbols indicate changes of location and situation: a waving blue flag signifies the sea; a painted wall, an entire city; a black flag denotes a storm; a red wheel is a wagon.

A scene from the Beijing Opera.

Antiquity – Present

This photograph of a scene from a Nō drama demonstrates all the classical elements of the genre. The empty stage is decorated with the obligatory (divine) fir tree; the musicians and chorus take their place on the stage along with the actors. The emotional climax—here the appearance of a jealous female spirit—is portrayed in dance.

The Japanese Nō play—A voyage into the past

In the Nō play we can admire the rare phenomenon of a genre that has remained unchanged for 500 years. In the 14th century, the actor Kaname reformed the *sarugaku*, the traditional dramatic form of both court and commoners. Within three generations, his family had created almost the entire Nō repertoire of 3,000 pieces, about 200 of which have survived.

At the center of the short Nō play are persons who do not want to let go of the material world after their death, and who must therefore return to the scenes of their former passions. Normally, five pieces are presented in an evening—one play each about the gods, the struggle of warriors, women, and fate, and a concluding piece. The plays are separated by comic interludes, called *kyōgen*.

The secret of the Japanese mask

Unlike the painted masks of the *kabuki* theater, the Nō masks are plain, but they exude a

Nō masks replace the individual expression of the actors with the objective expression of the role. Numerous female masks appear, along with gods and ghosts—although only males played female roles until the 19th century.

mysterious power. Before the performance, the actor, to try to forge a complete identification with his mask, meditates intensely on its appearance. There is a Japanese saying that "a good mask moves its actor," rather than the reverse. Thus, the actor supposedly experiences the play as a person experiences life.

Historically, the Nō drama served the aesthetic and meditatively oriented Japanese military nobility as the artistic expression of Buddhism. The drama is highly concentrated, simple and slow. The strongly symbolic gestures and movements follow the predetermined choreography down to minute detail: the position of the feet is supposed to reveal character; a hand before the eyes indicates weeping; a search is signified by a slight turning of the head. The one universal prop is the fan, which can symbolize everything from wings to water.

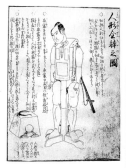

Jôruri: Popular puppet drama, unchanged since the 18th century. Operated by up to three puppeteers, each figure is a masterwork of carving capable of movement by not only all ten fingers but also eyelids and eyebrows.

Antiquity – Present

A short lexicon of Japanese theater

Aragoto: a macho-bravura style of acting in a Kabuki drama, using expansive movements, oversized costumes and wigs, and symbolically painted masks

Angura: underground Japanese theater from the 1968 student revolt. Trivial or folkloric motifs are employed for radical social criticism.

Butō: experimental dance movement from the 1950s that broke with the stagnant traditional forms.

Kagura, Gigaku, Bugaku: dance and masked dramas from China and Korea, celebrated since ca. 1000 A.D. at the royal court and in Shinto temples.

Kyōgen: a comic interlude during a Nō production.

Mie: *Kabuki* tableau: all movement is frozen at the emotional climax.

Sarugaku: a generic term for various court and temple entertainments performed by magicians, jugglers, and other artists; it developed in the 14th century into more serious dramatic presentations and is the source of the more artistic Nō drama.

Shimpa: a form of spoken drama that became a forum for the spread of liberal ideas in the 19th century; elements of traditional Japanese drama were incorporated into a European dramatic framework.

Shingeti: a "new theater" of the 20th century, renouncing traditional forms and concentrating on modern world theater.

Shite: the chief actor in a Nō drama, accompanied by a supporting player (*waki*), a retinue (*tsure*), and chorus.

Kabuki: the actor Otani Oniji at the end of the 18th century.

Kabuki theater

Over the centuries, the high poetry of the Nō theater was the exclusive domain of the aristocratic cognoscente. But the rising merchant class in the 17th century brought with it a new moneyed class that turned to a new theatrical form for entertainment.

Kabuki theater first mounted the stage as pure dance theater; its erotic presentation of women and boys guaranteed popular success. In the mid-17th century performances were prohibited, probably as an attempt to forestall the leveling of class distinctions between the Samurai and the rich bourgeois citizens. But the kabuki theater quickly resurrected itself in another form by shamelessly appropriating all the glamor of contemporary crowd pleasers. From the popular puppet theater *Jôruri*, the new kabuki borrowed both the content and the stage shape, and from the Nō tradition gorgeous costumes. As in the Chinese musical plays, at the center of kabuki theater stands a single virtuoso artist, who became a kind of cult star in the 1600s. With his mastery of music ("ka"), acrobatic dance ("bu"), as well as drama ("ki"), he crafted a kind of

musical revue. At the apotheosis of the play—always based on a stirring dramatic portayal of a basic human emotion such as hate, love, or jealousy—the movement freezes into a tableau

Even in its early years, *Kabuki* drama was produced in theater buildings, which also served as restaurants. The elaborate use of changing stage decoration, equipment to lower the stage, flying machines, and revolving panels is not unlike the stage machinery of the European baroque theater.

("mie"), while the actor's delivery changes into an artificial screaming or sobbing. At this point the audience is supposed to cry in response, "This is what we were waiting for!"

Kabuki theater borrowed heavily from Japan's longstanding *bunraku* puppet theater, while the puppet theater equally turned to kabuki for inspiration and technique. Today, kabuki actors strive to imbue the tradition with a contemporary flavor. Where historical themes were used to convey political criticism in the 18th century, today experiments with rock music may draw a young audience. The colors of the painted masks and the strictly prescribed acrobatics still serve as a symbolic language, but everything else—the costumes, stage structure, and technical effects—is changing to meet a changing public.

The plot may be illogical and unreal, and the figures grotesque, but the tableau-like presentation of feelings must touch the audience's heart.

Antiquity – Present

Onnagata: a female *Kabuki* figure played by a male.

The red facial lines of this *Aragoto* denote a positive hero; brown-violet lines would signify a ghost, and blue a villain. The classical *Aragoto* costume is grotesquely enlarged, corresponding to the expansive choreography.

33

800	Charlemagne is crowned emperor of the Holy Roman Empire
1096–99	The first Crusade
1163	Construction begins on the Cathedral of Notre Dame in Paris
ca. 1230	Guillaume de Laris, *Le Roman de la Rose*
1252	Introduction of torture by the Inquisition
1253	Foundation of the University of Paris (the Sorbonne)
1290	Expulsion of the Jews from England and France
1321	Dante Alighieri, *The Divine Comedy*
1339	Start of 100 Years' War between England and France
1348	The first epidemic of plague claims the lives of one-third of Europe's population
1388	Geoffrey Chaucer, *The Canterbury Tales*
1433	English replaces French and Latin as the official language of the court in England
1484	Papal Bull against witches

800 – 1600

Spiritual and secular power were inseparably linked in the Middle Ages: Emperor Henry IV (illustration of ca. 1115).

The culture of Christendom

In the Middle Ages the rise of numerous new states radically altered the structure of Europe. The decline of trade and commerce after the fall of Rome had fostered the development of locally based feudal economies. The citizenry of the cities, which had been the bearer of culture in antiquity, lost not only their political, but their cultural significance. The new civilization in western Europe, a fusion of the ancient and Germanic traditions, was dominated by the Christian Church. In a process that lasted through almost the entire medieval period, the Church was now in a position to conquer from above, often literally with fire and sword, rather than from below as it had in its early days.

Under the hegemony of the Church, medieval citizens saw themselves as Christians rather than as members of society in a modern sense. The Church was active in every area of public and social life, from the legislation of inheritance and the restitution of stolen property to the banning of adultery, perjury, and usury (that is, any profit accruing from money transactions). Philosophy itself, along with the other sciences, was declared to be nothing more than the hand-maiden of theology.

Any move-ment that tried to carve a place for itself outside Church control met with hostile treatment and, in the late Middle Ages, bloody persecution at the hands of the Inquisition. Witch trials served to extirpate the remains of heathendom and magical consciousness; the persecution of heretics rooted out reform movements within the Church.

800 – 1600

Church patriarch Saint Augustine of Hippo (354–430) described in detail the evil effect of theater in his *Confessions*: "I have sinned indeed, my Lord and my God. ... Not desiring to choose the better, I was disobedient, and from a love of foolish pastimes and the desire to win proudly at tournaments; and I let my ears be tempted with poetic legends so that they became ever desirous to hear more, and I ever more desirous to attend the theater and rivet my eyes on classic drama." In this detail from a medieval manuscript of *The City of God*, the scribe is throwing an eraser at a mouse.

Mummery, music, and dance were the chief elements of popular entertainment.

At courtly social events, the German Minnesang was cultivated; here, the troubadour Heinrich the Woman Praiser.

800 – 1600

Dancing jester.

The subculture of the Middle Ages: Wandering players

Less brutally but no less energetically, the Church suppressed drama. During the entire medieval period, traveling players, acrobats, and musicians stood under Church proscription, less because of the drama's heathen origins than because of its immorality and shamelessness.

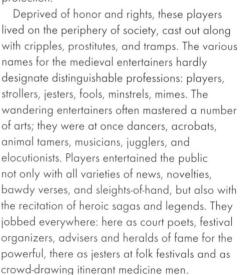

Nevertheless, even in the medieval world, clowns and fools held their place as emblems of the grotesque and the animalistic—a counterbalance to the divine order of the world—and were eagerly received at annual markets, in the courts of nobles, and even in monasteries. Officially itinerants, they stood outside Church control—but also outside any protection.

Deprived of honor and rights, these players lived on the periphery of society, cast out along with cripples, prostitutes, and tramps. The various names for the medieval entertainers hardly designate distinguishable professions: players, strollers, jesters, fools, minstrels, mimes. The wandering entertainers often mastered a number of arts; they were at once dancers, acrobats, animal tamers, musicians, jugglers, and elocutionists. Players entertained the public not only with all varieties of news, novelties, bawdy verses, and sleights-of-hand, but also with the recitation of heroic sagas and legends. They jobbed everywhere: here as court poets, festival organizers, advisers and heralds of fame for the powerful, there as jesters at folk festivals and as crowd-drawing itinerant medicine men.

Flute player and juggling boy.

The Church as educator

In the long run, there is not a religion in the world that can avoid performing rituals. This is especially true when a religion develops from a secret rite for the initiated to a politically significant state institution, and moreover when it wishes to propagandize its new teaching as quickly as possible.

The medieval populace was largely illiterate and still followed the magical practices that were a part of its folk culture. The Church incorporated these customs into its liturgical calendar and exploited them to spread the Christian faith. Thus, Christmas supplanted the heathen celebration of the sun god, *sol invictus*, at the end of December; today's Easter bunnies and egg hunts originated in pagan spring and fertility rituals.

Once it seemed that the danger of any widespread return to heathen cults was past, the Church, like other religions, accepted into its service theatrical rituals involving the use of incense, candles, and blessed ointments. Motivated by the increasing need to grasp the holy with all five senses and to represent it aesthetically, the Church finally yoked graphic and theatrical arts to its program of liturgical education.

The dramatization of the liturgy

When the Council of Constantinople (692 A.D.) ordered the humanizing of the divinity, the Church relaxed its prohibition against pictures and began to stage embellishments to the Easter service. The insertion of antiphonal hymns sung by a chorus and soloist, and of tropes, or textual expansions of the liturgical songs, was intended to illustrate the teachings of the Church. On Good Friday, the cross was taken from the altar, draped in a shroud, and carried in a procession

800 – 1600

Art in the Middle Ages served effectively to promote religion. The brutal scenes of the Massacre of the Innocents at Bethlehem were a favorite of religious painters.

The apostles racing to the sepulcher.

from the church to the cemetery. The raising of the cross again on Easter reenacted the resurrection of Christ.

The first dramatic roles, played by costumed priests, are to be found in the confrontation between the three Marys and the angel at the empty tomb of Christ. Soon burlesque made its way into the Easter liturgy when the apostle Peter engaged in a race with John to the sepulcher and the three Marys were held up by a talkative tradesman as they tried to buy holy ointment for Christ's corpse. The latter scene was expanded into an independent *merchant's play* in which the young wife of a haggling charlatan clearly dallies with his apprentice, Rubin.

Religious drama

It was only a small step from dramatic additions to the liturgy to more complex biblical plays, which spread throughout the Christian world and drew the congregation into the performance.

In order to dramatize the liturgy, crucifixes were constructed with removable Christ figures.

In addition to Christmas and Easter plays, an amazing variety of themes and forms have survived. *Miracle plays* depict the lives and wondrous deeds of saints while *prophet* and *Antichrist plays* conjure up the

battle between heaven and hell on Judgment Day. In *donkey and child-bishop burlesques*, children and adults act out the roles of religious officials in unruly mockery of Church ceremonies.

By moving away from liturgy, the plays were freed from the constraints of rigorously symbolic dramatization. From the Christ who had been present only as a symbol in the first Easter dramas, a character capable of speech and action was developed for the sake of increased emotional realization. By the 13th century, the plays had spilled out of the church to the plaza in front of the church, and were no longer sung in Latin, but were now spoken in the vernacular. There was, however, no true secularization in this displacement; rather, the Church was stepping out into the broader world of the new, self-confident, middle-class citizenry of the growing medieval metropolises.

The Marys with the ointment seller.

800 – 1600

Mystery and passion plays

The movement away from the confines of the church building suggested a broadening of theatrical content and production possibilities. Countless settings could be constructed around and in the middle of the open space in front of the church. Performances were no longer limited to a single theme, but took on the whole of salvation history from the creation of the world to the Last Judgment. God the Father could be enthroned on a podium on the church portal. The opposite side of the plaza lent itself to a three-

Plan of the staging area for a passion play (Villingen, Germany) showing the locations of the playing positions.

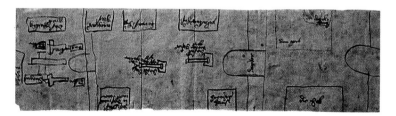

The Lucerne Easter Play of 1583 is a typical example of the use of the entire market-place. The role assignments mirrored the social hierarchy of the city: patricians and guild members played the most important parts, while servants appeared in minor roles.

800 – 1600

dimensional mouth of hell from which Christ could dramatically rescue the biblical patriarchs on Judgment Day. The devils who combed through the audience at the end of a play on a hunt for souls brought to life the essence of evil.

While performances of *mystery* or *passion plays* may have created emotional tension, they also provided for an entertaining relaxation of tensions by bringing holy events to life. After all, on His journey from Heaven to Hell, the Savior had to pass through the world. The stations of Christ's passion and death often formed the center of the mystery cycle. During the production, all the settings and characters were present simultaneously; as the public moved from scaffold to scaffold, it was presented with the entire order of creation and salvation history. In order to fill all the roles required by the festivals, which could last for days or even weeks, lay citizens (that is, men) began to join the clergy in the performances until, in the 14th century, the entire production was handed over to the guilds and the lay brotherhoods. Now the plays were staged in the

This stage plan of Valenciennes (1547) depicts a straight row of individual scenes ranging from heaven to the mouth of hell. Viewers and players not involved in the action sat under tent roofs on solid rising rows of chairs directly facing the stage.

marketplace and were financed by the city.

The great mystery cycles were no longer a demonstration of the power of the Church and became instead a focal point of civic culture. As they spread throughout the continent, especially into the Alps, Flanders, and France, various regional traditions developed.

The Passion Play of Valenciennes lasted 25 days, and has survived in the form of numerous painted miniatures. This one shows the Visit of the Three Kings, the Flight into Egypt, the Massacre of the Innocents, and the suicide of Herod.

800 – 1600

A new relation to reality

The late medieval passion plays brought a significant change in the veneration of Christ. In place of the glory of His resurrection, Christ's humiliation and suffering form the center of the dramatization. The Passion of Christ mirrored the new consciousness of 14th-century society, struggling with economic decline, hunger, the plague, and crises in religious and secular authorities.

Like the graphic arts, the theater of the late Middle Ages focused more and more on empirical reality. The aim was to shore up the truth of Church doctrine with impressive theatrical effects. Imaginative and effective productions were made possible by an array of stage machinery

A *mystery play* on the martyrdom of the blessed Apollonia: at right is the director with open playbook and director's staff, and the mouth of hell, filled with devils; in the background, heaven is reached by a ladder.

800 – 1600

that allowed for flight and descent, manna that fell from heaven, water miracles, and true-to-life torture scenes. Blood flowed richly from animal-skin balloons concealed under gowns and wigs—until that point in the play when the actor was replaced by a wax mannequin that was then subjected to a dramatically detailed martyrdom—quartering, disemboweling, decapitation, and more.

The tendency toward increasing realism strengthened the spectacular components of drama at the cost of the religious. In the 16th century, as the Middle Ages were winding down and the arts and ideas of the Renaissance were filtering throughout Europe, the Catholic Church and, above all, the new reformed churches forbade the increasingly imaginative plays; this measure aimed also at permanently suppressing popular theatrical culture, which was by now taking on a life and a momentum of its own.

Secular drama

It was not until the late Middle Ages that secular dramatic forms developed within the framework of seasonal folk festivals. In France, the most important comic forms, *farce* and *sotie*, originally made their appearance only during the pre-Lenten carnival. These skits provided a critical and satirical look at everyday life, and did not

Folk theater at the *Boerenkermes*, by **Pieter Breughel the Younger**, adapted from Pieter Balten.

Glossary
Morality play: allegorical drama in which abstract ideas and properties—such as the struggle between human virtue and vice—are personified.
Mystery play: open-air theatrical staging of biblical stories, particularly common in England and France.
Passion play: an Easter drama that stretched over several days to include the passion of Christ, usually interrupted by profane interludes.
Shrovetide play: a loose arrangement of coarsely comic secular scenes concerning adultery and lawsuits; developed for the carnival in the 15th century.
Spiritual play: religious drama growing out of liturgical antiphony; the oldest topic is the Easter play, followed by Christmas, prophet, Corpus Christi, Last Judgment, miracle, Antichrist, and paradise plays.

shy away from using grotesque comic distortion to ridicule both church and state authorities. While the farce in medieval France depicted the "real" world in a short situation-comedy-like manner, the sotie had scarcely any claim to plot or structure, but involved a standard array of fools, clods, "sots," dressed in a cap with ass's ears, engaged in often vulgar banter. They also relied on acrobatics and a medieval brand of slapstick.

Like the French farce, the German *Fastnachtsspiel* (Shrove Tuesday play) splintered off from the annual carnival and established itself as an independent drama in the courtyards of inns and in marketplaces. The uninhibited sexual and scatological humor of the urban craft guilds was mostly at the expense of peasants, women, and Jews, but particularly enjoyed taking potshots at the vices of the clergy and nobility.

The more serious English *morality play*, which allegorized the clash between vice and virtue, survives today in *Everyman* (first printed ca. 1510–25), the most-produced play of European theater history. The happy-go-lucky Everyman is ordered by the rather godfatherly Death to appear before the throne of God. Everyman begs in vain for his boon companions, among whom are Friendship, Kindred, and Riches, to stand by him. But even his Good Deeds are too weak to accompany him, and advise him to repent and atone. Strengthened at last, he goes on his way to death.

800 – 1600

The most important author of the German carnival play is Hans Sachs (1494–1576). As chief of the Meistersingers, he wrote over 4,000 songs and 87 Shrovetide plays. Less obscene than many contemporary plays, his works evince a tendency toward moral didacticism.

Since 1920, the Salzburg Festival (established in 1917) has opened with a production of *Jedermann* (*Everyman*) by Hugo von Hofmannsthal in front of the cathedral. (This photo shows a 1973 staging with Curt Jürgens in the leading role.)

43

"I can take any empty space and call it a bare stage. A man walks across this empty space whilst someone else is watching him, and this is all that is needed for an act of theatre to be engaged."

So begins *The Empty Space*, by Peter Brook, one of the dominant theater directors and thinkers of the latter 20th century. Theater has been and is performed everywhere: in streets and plazas under the open skies; in churches, palaces, and tents; in the simplicity of inn court-yards and the splendor of opera houses—and it has recently moved into such workaday spaces as classrooms, buses, and factories.

Theater has always been a form of communication—between humans and gods, between actors and viewers. It can happen anywhere an audience can gather. Theater's so-cial function in a given culture or epoch will help redefine the relation-ship between players and audience, influencing the nature of the space where theater is played, and in particular the relationship between the stage and the place for the audience.

Ritualistic cult theater takes place under the open sky. The viewers gather in a circle, in the center of which the priest-actors dance around a sacrificial altar. Not only does everyone's position offer an equally good view, but in one glance each member of the audience can take in the rest of the audience as well.

In the oldest reconstructable stage form of Europe—the highly devel-oped theater of ancient Greece—the central arena of action was known as the orchestra. The *theatron*, or viewing area, spread out in rising levels into the surrounding hillside. The audience watching the songs and dances in honor of Dionysus ex-perienced the performance as a community ritual vitally binding to-gether mythology, religion, and nature.

As Greek drama developed, the small wooden plat-form (*proskenion*) located in the rear third of the orchestra increased in impor-tance. Toward the back of this plat-form, the *skene*, a shed with several

The amphitheater of Epidaurus is the best preserved of the ancient Greek theaters.

The Roman theater in Orange with *cavea* and *scaenae frons*.

doors, allowed costume changes and entrances.

Although the theaters of imperial Rome were patterned after Greek models, Roman theater construction reveals the very different social purpose of drama in ancient Rome. No longer a religious celebration or a national political instrument, Roman theater served to entertain and divert the populace, and also to impress upon it the power of its tyrants. The Roman masters ordered the construction of multistory, ornamented theater buildings. The front of the stage area, the *scaenae frons*, was raised and decorated, while the orchestra shrank into the half-circular *cavea*, where the more privileged members of the public were seated directly before the stage. The seating arrangements, with unequal views of the stage, no longer reflected a democratic relation among the citizens but the class structure of the Roman society.

Disconnected in both form and content from ancient theater, the ubiquitous religious plays of the Middle Ages developed their own unique *simultaneous stage*. Scaffold stages for the various Bible stories were built next to one another in a row or half-circle, originally inside the church building, later in front of the church or in the marketplace. During the passion or mystery play, the public moved from one platform stage to another, while lay actors repeated their scenes amid three-dimensional stage decorations such as the mouth of hell, the throne of God, and various earthly stations in between. The simultaneous stage is symbolic of the total Christian cosmos—of the simultaneous presence of earth, heaven, and hell. As in most theater that grows out of religious ritual, the audience was meant to understand itself as a part of this cosmos as it moved among the stations.

In England, settings were constructed on pageant wagons. The audience stood in place while wagons carried the performances to it, one after another, in a kind of festival procession. To bridge the intervals while the wagons were being moved, mounted "stage managers" explained the dramatic action.

45

In addition to religious and state forms of theater, we also have evidence of traveling troupes of players who, since antiquity, have entertained the public with a secular repertoire. Greek mimes and medieval jugglers, like the actors of the *commedia dell'arte* and "street theater" today, have long made do by quickly throwing together a few boards to create an ad-hoc platform stage. If necessary, the rear could be strung with a curtain to create a dressing room or to enable more effective entrances and exits. Lacking the scenery and technical effects typical of Roman, and particularly medieval, theater, the play depends entirely on the talent of the players. This kind of theater is particularly marked by the proximity of the actors to their audience, which stands on three sides of the scaffold and could be addressed directly.

Corral stage.

The booth stage, often erected in the courtyards of inns, became the model in 17th-century England and Spain for the first commercial theaters—the Shakespearean stage (as we now think of it) and the Spanish *corrales*. In these open-air theaters, the partially roofed stage extended forward into the audience area; a ballustraded dressing hut closed the stage from behind and offered further possibilities for staging (the "arras," often cited in the rare Shakespearean stage directions). Scenes were set by a few spoken

Itinerant stage.

words or a piece of movable scenery. The ordinary members of the public stood at the foot of the stage, while the richer citizens and nobles sat in the surrounding galleries.

The removal of theater to enclosed areas during the Renaissance launched a new era in theater design, producing concepts that have been accepted as the "classical stage" for nearly 400 years. European princes, eager to display their greatness, welcomed the theater as an enrichment to their grandiose court feasts. The newly rediscovered art and architecture of Greece and Rome provided the model for stage and theater design.

A first effort of the new humanists was to reconstruct the comic stage of Terence. Like a row of old-fashioned bathing cabanas, individual curtained cells, separated by walls and small columns, stood adjacent to each other behind a narrow stage. A sign placed above each cell identified it as a specific location; the actors had only to emerge from the appropriate cells and deliver their dialogue. The action moved from one location to another, as in the simultaneous staging of the Middle Ages, but without violating the classical principle of the unities of time, place, and action.

The first Renaissance stages were merely temporary structures assembled in banquet halls, but before long permanent theaters were erected in the palaces. The earliest sur-

Terence stage.

viving example of a closed theater in Europe is the *Teatro Olimpico* in Vicenza, designed by Andrea Palladio based strictly on the rediscovered classical architectural studies of Vitruvius (building began in 1579 and was completed after Palladio's death by Vincenzo Scamozzi in 1585). The audience area enclosed the orchestra, which now provided space for the musicians, in a half-ellipse and for the first time in theater history could be darkened. A colonnade of Corinthian columns and statues adorned the theater's rounded rear wall, while the ceiling was painted to resemble the heavens and to give the illusion of an open-air theater. Behind the broad shallow stage a richly decorated wall with three classical arches functioned as a Roman *scaenae frons*. The arches opened up on painted perspectival views of streets disappearing into the distance.

The new art of perspectival painting provided the decisive impulses for the movement from the classical

Scaenae frons from the Teatro Olimpico.

imitations of the Renaissance to the baroque stage. In the first half of the 16th century, the stage was divided into a wide front acting area and a perspectivally painted, strongly sloped illusory stage. The angular framework of the painted walls was not strictly a scene setting, but rather an unchangeable stage decoration.

The next development was the perspectival stage with changeable stage settings. *Telari*, three-sided prisms with painted panels, were set in pairs on each side of the stage and turned to allow swift changes of scene. The *Teatro Farnese* in Parma (1618) was the first theater to use changeable settings—these were flat, painted walls that were rolled from beneath the stage and pushed into place. The auditorium of the baroque theater was divided according to strict hierarchical social divisions: the theater was ringed with galleries, whose levels, or tiers, were subdivided into separate loges. The cheapest seats with the

worst view of the stage were in the top row. The loge on the first level directly opposite the stage offered the best view of the perspectival stage back wall, and was correspondingly appointed as the court loge for princes.

Although the playing area no longer extended into the audience, the separation between the public and the stage was still not absolute. Changes of scene often took place on the open stage. Symmetry and formality characterized stage architecture, set arrangements, the social castes of characters, their movements and gestures. The stage, corresponding to the baroque world picture, symbolized deception and pretense, and hence the transience of the world. As the educated bourgeoisie appropriated the theater, its entry halls, stairs, and foyers acquired architectural significance as a locus for the self-dramatization of emancipated citizens. The ranking system of the court theaters was adapted by the new bourgeois management to the new social conditions, and the worst seats in the side loges and upper levels were eliminated altogether.

Not until the 19th century, the age of precise scientific research and a positivistic understanding of art, were the staggered set paintings replaced by realistic three-dimensional settings. Moving these bulky structures quickly required complex stage machinery such as turntable

stages, lifting and lowering apparatuses, and large transport wagons.
The stage curtain could conceal the
scene changes in order not to
breach the sought-after illusion of a
self-sufficient stage reality. The new
three-sided "peep-show" stage, with
its imaginary fourth wall toward the
audience, still defines conventional
theater architecture today. The advent of film, however, whose unlimit-
ed possibilities for realism have rendered stage "realism" ridiculous,
and attempts to achieve it superfluous, has inspired new concepts of
theater, and new ideas about what
constitutes a theater space. Theater
designers are rediscovering that it is
the physical presence of players
that gives theater its special commu-
nicative quality. Technology has
changed the face of the theater, just
as it has changed most aspects of
modern life. It has not, however, so
much dictated new forms of theater
space, as it has served the already
widening vision of theater directors.
Scenery changes that once required
manual labor may now be accom-
plished according to the crucial element of design, by computer-con-
trolled machinery, lighting changes,
image projections, and a myriad of
special effects. It is easy enough,
though, to distinguish between technology as gimmickry and technology as theatrical innovation. Most
new modern theaters are, above all,
flexible, and while their shape and
orientation, and the arrangement of

Baroque panel stage.

the audience seats as well as the
number of seats that can be accom-
modated can be changed easily
with the help of technology, directors
are just as likely to direct the actors
themselves to serve as stagehands to
move light and portable stage sets
and props or to dress stagehands in
costumes to suit the dramatic milieu.
In fact, the versatility of the modern
theater has opened up vast new
possibilities, not only for staging new
works but for reinterpreting, and re-
exploring the traditions of past
centuries. In this sense, the theater
space is now more than ever an
integral part of a theatrical statement. The "fourth wall" has been re-
opened to allow direct communication with the audience. The Shakespearean stage now acts as god-
father to contemporary arena
stages. We have even seen, as Peter
Brook presaged, modern and vari-
able stages being set up outside the
traditional temple of the muses.

1450 – 1600

ca. 1450 Gutenberg invents the printing press with movable type

1453 After the fall of Constantinople, Greek scholars fleeing to Italy bring texts of classical antiquity

1454 Peace of Lodi

1459 Foundation of a new Platonic Academy

1486 First printing of Vitruvius's *Ten Books of Architecture*

1492 Columbus discovers the New World

1498 Discovery of the sea passage to India

1503 Leonardo da Vinci paints the *Mona Lisa*

1507 Nicolaus Copernicus describes the heliocentric solar system

1508–12 Michelangelo paints the ceiling of the Sistine Chapel

1517 Martin Luther nails his 95 Theses on the church wall in Wittenberg

1525 Peasants' War in Germany

1527 Emperor Charles V sacks Rome

1533 Henry VIII declares himself head of the Church of England

1572 St. Bartholomew's Night massacre of 10,000 Huguenots

1588 Opera experiments by the Camerata Fiorentina

1600 Giordano Bruno is burned as a heretic

1607 Claudio Monteverdi: *Orfeo*

1633 Galileo Galilei renounces his "error" of the sun-centered solar system before the Inquisition court

The discovery and conquest of the New World would not have been possible without the technical achievements of the Renaissance. But the newly gained knowledge also led to great social and economic changes in Europe, and to the overturning of the old medieval world picture.

Entry into a new world

The modern age began with a series of landmark discoveries in geography, the natural sciences, and the humanities. Seafarers like Christopher Columbus explored unknown lands and seas, while Copernicus revolutionized astronomy (as Galileo would later overturn religion and philosophy) with the assertion that the sun, not the Earth, was the center of the solar system. The invention of the pocket watch in 1500 altered mankind's understanding of time, and the invention of the printing press offered heretofore unimaginable possibilities for the dissemination of new ideas.

With the development of early capitalism, the rise of secular authority spelled the end of the hegemony of the medieval Church. The Reformation brought about the greatest crisis in the history of the Church, while Italian humanism disseminated a new worldly attitude throughout Europe.

In the universities, the search for knowledge was disentangling itself from the dictates of faith; optimistically, scholars began the first attempts to explain the world on the basis of empirical observation. Philosophy, like art, turned its attention to mankind and stressed the freedom of the personality. The Renaissance, literally a rebirth of the thought and art of the ancient world, was not only a result of these developments, but a driving force behind them.

Court festivals and bourgeois letters

The newly awakened enthusiasm for the culture of the ancient world led in the 15th century to a new theater that was independent from the Church and its ritualistic motifs. At the same time that the laity of the towns was taking the mystery plays into their own hands, a new elite culture, far removed from both folklore and ritual, started to blossom in the courts and academies of Europe.

Renaissance theater differed from the theater that immediately preceded it in that it was understood as pure art, serving no purpose but to edify its public. Two important developments paved the way for this change in concept. In the theater of the humanists we can recognize the first tendencies toward seeing ancient classical drama

as a verbal art in which a tightly constructed plot is advanced by means of dialogue. The triumph of this new literary genre was accompanied by an understanding of the stage as a finite space in which the locations of the action no longer need simultaneously to be physically located next to one another, but can follow one another according to chronological changes of scene.

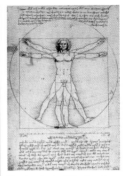

The *Anatomical Studies* of **Leonardo da Vinci** (1452–1519) display the prevalent Renaissance interest in the nature of things and their precise representation. The life work of the artist, who was at once a painter, architect, sculptor, technician, and scientist, is representative of the universal educational ideal of humanism.

1450 – 1600

The adoption of ancient classical materials and forms by the Renaissance was strongest in painting and architecture. The artists became important partners in the renewal of the theater. Thus, the Teatro Olimpico in Vicenza (built in 1579–85 by Andrea Palladio and Vincenzo Scamozzi), with its amphitheater-like auditorium and architectonically richly decorated stage back wall, was built according to Roman models.

This detail from the title page of a 15th-century edition of a Terence work demonstrates how the medieval artist imagined the antique world. The poet, surrounded by his audience, is reciting the work, while masked mimes illustrate the events with gestures.

While it is true that the much-admired classical drama had been discovered before the 15th century—Seneca and Terence were also a part of medieval Latin instruction—every sense of classical production had been lost. It was the humanistic scholars whose eager study of dramatic texts and architectural descriptions of Roman theaters enabled the rehabilitation of classical dramas.

The pomp-loving producers of courtly festivals were always looking for new attractions for their programs, and they took to the new "classical wave" enthusiastically. Soon after the first Latin productions were held before scholarly audiences in Rome, the Duke Ercole I d'Este arranged for an Italian presentation of Plautus's *Menaechmi* in 1486 at the court of Ferrara. In contrast to the idealized scholarly productions, which strove primarily to produce an exact reconstruction of the originals, at court the chief value was magnificence of production—or *spectacle*. The Duke of Ferrara is supposed to have invested a stately one thousand gold ducats for costumes and stage effects for the first performance.

Bernardo Buontalenti, costume designs for the *Intermediae* of the great theater festival of the Medici, presented in the Teatro degli Uffizi in Florence, 1589.

Scholastic comedy

While the court of Ferrara, with its annual presentations, was the first brilliant center for the resurrection of ancient comedy, the dukedom's art-sensitive princes also supported the creation of *commedia erudita*, a vernacular comedy written by academics and scholars. In 1508, Ariosto's *La Cassaria* (The chest) was first presented. Ariosto, who had already made a name for himself as translator of Plautus and Terence, at first conformed strictly to his classical teachers. In addition to the five-act division, he also co-opted situations and characters from the Latin comedies and set his plays in ancient Rome.

In his second drama, *I suppositi*, Ariosto transplanted a classic theme into the world of the 15th century, and allowed himself satiric jibes at his contemporaries. The poet-cardinal Bernardo Dovizi Bibbiena went a step further and dared to place erotic motifs from popular novellas in his comedy *Calandria*.

In *Mandragola*, an amusing defense of adulterous relations, the political philosopher Niccoló Machiavelli, best known for his tract on political expedience and justification, *The Prince*, broke entirely with classical models and drew a sharp portrait of the customs, especially the vices, of his age. The play remains today the most-produced comedy of the Italian Renaissance.

The huge demand for new texts for the *commedia erudita*, which was at first thoroughly popular, summoned forth many, but unfortunately clearly less talented imitators of Ariosto and Machiavelli.

Under their pens, "school" comedies calcified into a genre frozen with mechanistic style and utterly boring. Thus, the brisk lively types of the commedia dell'arte, a new impromptu comic play developed by professional players and

Ludovico Ariosto (1474–1533) spent the largest portion of his life at the court of Ferrara where he was in charge of a small court theater and served as a poet, actor, and director.

1450 – 1600

Niccoló Machiavelli (1469–1527) was the most influential political thinker of his day, and won his place in history not as a dramatist, but as author of the politically realistic textbook for the absolute ruler, *The Prince*.

The beginnings of professional theater are found among the works of amateur dramatists such as Angelo Beolco, known as Ruzzante, who wrote and produced comedies with a small troupe of players in manor houses and at the court of Ferrara. With his development of stereotyped characters, Ruzzante was a pioneer in the effective staging of "learned" comedy, thus opening the way to the commedia dell'arte.

A scene from Bernardo Dovizi Bibbiena's *Calandria*.

performers with a multitude of skills, stole the show from the more staid *commedia erudita*.

"De casibus" tragedy

Tragedy was not terribly successful during the Renaissance. For one thing, it was ill-suited to the cheerful extravagance and spectacle that were desired by the pompous court festivals. Greek tragedy was at most a pastime of scholars in their towers.

Where Aeschylus, Sophocles, and Euripides grew musty in limbo, the dramas of the Roman Seneca were viewed by his Italian descendants as the culmination of classical tragedy. A small coterie of dramatists attempted the unpopular genre, but aside from the *Orazia* by the notorious satirist Aretino, nothing of interest to theatrical history was produced.

The lack of attention accorded to Greek tragedy was balanced by keen theoretical interest in the ancient Greek philosopher Aristotle, whose *Poetics*, translated into Latin in 1536, defined the

"With a goose quill and a few pieces of paper, I mock the world." The feared satirist Pietro Aretino (1492–1556), the "scourge of the princes," was the first professional author of his time. Many consider his drama *L'Orazia* the best tragedy of the 16th century.

humanistic poetic norms that were to rule the theater in Italy and in particular France for centuries—this despite the fact (as modern scholarship has clarified) that the *Poetics* were intended to be descriptive of tragedy, not prescriptive or proscriptive, that Aristotle was reflecting on tragedy as he had experienced it, and not attempting to set any standards for all time.

Among the most important "rules" was that of the three unities of place, action, and time. These unities require that characters move only within a limited space (if at all—there are few scene changes in the Greek tragedies). The single direction of the action, in which all are involved—with no subplots muddling the unraveling of the central theme—must be laid out and resolved within the span of twenty-four hours.

The "law of the estates" reserved tragic consideration for the rise and fall of noble families and nations (the first estate); comedy, in contrast, focused exclusively on the more earthly tendencies of the third estate, the common people, at whose foibles it was considered acceptable to laugh. (This distinction was, of course, headed toward obsolescence in the more hybrid forms that would emerge in the later Renaissance.)

From pastoral drama to opera

The brief golden age of "scholastic" comedies and "de casibus" tragedies was soon outshone by the glittering victory march of a new genre that united comedy and tragedy. Until far into the 17th century, the backward-looking pastoral

One of the new stage forms of the Renaissance was the neutral bathing-cell stage of Terence. The narrow stage area was bordered toward the rear by closable curtains, creating cells or little cabins, from which the characters emerged to conduct dialogue. The row-like organization of the settings corresponded to the medieval simultaneous stage, but the new principle of the three unities of time, place, and action could now be observed.

Torquato Tasso (1544–95) introduced a new literary theatrical style with his pastoral play *Aminta*.

1450 – 1600

The scenery for a tragedy shows the elaborate houses of proper personages.

The "satyr scene" of a pastoral play included trees, rocks, fountains, flowers, and rural cottages. Such a landscape allowed creatures to live without restraint in the realm of nature.

drama ruled the court festivals and, in its imitation of the idyllic pastoral poetry of Virgil, inspired a longing for a halcyon age of harmony.

The location of the pastoral is the charming Arcadia, a woodland where Nature is at times a benevolent mother, at other times a malevolent obstacle. Arcadia is populated by nymphs, shepherds, and Olympian gods. In a complicated plot, Arcadian lovers find and lose each other before, in the face of a seemingly unavoidable catastrophe, they are finally united.

All the elements of classical pastoral poetics were used by Torquato Tasso in his *Aminta*, which was produced by Duke Alfonso II on the Po River island of Belvedere near Ferrara in 1573. The *Aminta* shares the reputation of a masterwork of its genre with Giovanni Battista Guarini's *Il Pastor Fido*.

The pastoral poets kept their distance from the political and social crises that shook the present day. Their backward-looking utopias acted as escapes into a beautiful, insubstantial world.

Today the pastoral drama is virtually unknown, except by students and scholars, and would be considered a mere anomaly in the history of world theater were it not for one thing: we have pastoral drama, in large measure, to thank for the birth of the opera. The *dramma per musica*, and with it, the new form

of the solo song were developed in imitation of the legendary classical art of declamation by modern musical and gesticular means. Pastoral drama, with its musical interludes, ballet, and choral singing, provided an ideal framework. The fantastic figures and settings of Arcadia offered additional rich possibilities for producing the new ostentatious theater of courtly display within an appropriate structure.

The preference for glamorous costumes and settings persists in some opera houses today, though the influence of minimalism, among many other trends over the centuries in the arts has fostered a modern aesthetic that makes such extravagance seem almost grotesque, alien, and anachronistic.

Claudio Monteverdi (1567–1643) united in *Orfeo* the pastoral play with the musical forms of his time into a new genre, opera.

Bourgeois houses prevail in the scenery for comedies.

1450 – 1600

Glossary

Commedia erudita: Italian Renaissance comedy based on a Roman model and classical subject matter; considered "erudite" because it was produced by learned authors based on academic formulations.

Humanistic drama: Latin drama based on a Roman model, using biblical and moral themes.

Intermedium: originally an interlude in a comedy performance; developed into an independent drama with highly complex staging conventions.

Jesuit theater: originally a Catholic school drama, developed into a general medium of counter-Reformation propaganda with opulent production.

Pastoral play: backward-looking genre of Renaissance theater, set in unrealistic and idealized world of shepherds.

School drama: humanistic drama used for pedagogical instruction.

Terence stage: specially designed single-setting stage, using "cabana" type bathing cells, developed for the dramas of Terence.

Trionfi: imitation of ancient Roman triumphal processions with elaborate pageant wagons, accompanied by dancers, musicians, and others.

The settings of school drama included college courtyards, schoolrooms, university rooms, city hall rooms, guild halls, dance floors, and open plazas. The stage was set up on barrels, as in this 1581 Laurentius play in Cologne, and required no special accoutrements.

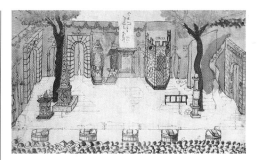

1450 – 1600

Theater of the schools

In the 16th century, the didactic usefulness of the theater was "discovered" by humanists. Performances of Latin plays were adopted into academic curricula in order to provide instruction for the performing pupils in Latin conversation and to foster their confidence in public appearance.

The objective of school drama was moral teaching, while the approach involved imitation of classical form, although what records survive suggest to us that the school plays were also influenced by medieval religious plays. Martin Luther himself expressly recommended theatrical plays for school instruction; moreover, he insightfully saw them as a suitable propagandistic tool for the Reformation.

In clear contradistinction from the medieval mystery cycles, school dramas worked up materials from biblical and classical stories and legends. These were freely reinterpreted in the spirit of the Reformation and, by the more aggressive of the authors, sprinkled with harsh attacks on the "papist" opponents.

One of the most important institutions of the Protestant school theater was the Strasbourg Latin School, which presented not only the most important authors of international humanistic drama, but also Plautus and Terence in Latin, and Aristophanes, Sophocles, and Euripides in

Martin Luther (1483–1546) was a decisive supporter of school theater. This portrait is by Lucas Cranach the Elder, 1529.

Greek. Pupils and teachers in Strasbourg are said to have been so enthusiastic that general instruction in more traditional modes paled by comparison.

It was only a matter of time before the Jesuits, exponents of the Catholic cause, adapted school theater as an important counter-Reformation medium. Jesuit drama addresses the heart of the public directly through spectacular stories concerning the virtues and vices of historical personages. These productions shone with the use of every theatrical device imaginable, and involved more than a hundred performers who appeared in dance and musical interludes. More visual than verbal, Jesuit drama was meant to enthrall the crowds of onlookers and to enlist them into the service of religious education and move them to wonder and fear. This sensual approach constituted the distinct difference between the drama of the Jesuits and the "antiart" productions of the Protestants. Music, ballet, and allegorical interludes were standard components of the Jesuit theater which, unlike the Reformation-oriented school theater, avoided direct attacks against religious opponents. The "moral" of the pieces reached a climax in the denouements suggesting that even the power of intelligence so valued by the Renaissance was finally a gift of God.

"The playing of comedy in the schools should not be forbidden for the sake of the boys, but allowed, first because they will practice Latin language, and furthermore so that the fine artistically drawn characters will instruct the populace and each person and class will be reminded and warned concerning what behavior belongs to a servant, a master, an apprentice and the aged—what is due and how he should behave. Yes indeed, the office and duties will be held on high and presented before the eyes of all dignitaries, how each person in his estate should behave in outward conduct as in a mirror." (Martin Luther, *Table Talk*).

1450 – 1600

A scene from Johann Rasser's *Play of Child Raising*, 1574.

1579 The Netherlands wins the struggle for independence from the Spanish Habsburg monarchy

1588 England defeats the Spanish Armada

1598 Spain recognizes acting as a legal profession

1605 Miguel de Cervantes, Don Quixote

1618–48 Thirty Years War

1620 Pilgrims land with the Mayflower on the coast of New England

1624 Martin Opitz, Book of German Poetry

1637 The Teatro di San Cassiano, the first permanent opera house, opens in Venice

1640 Scenery as stage decoration spreads throughout Europe

1642 Rembrandt van Rijn paints The Nightwatch

1651 Thomas Hobbes' Leviathan argues the submission of the individual to the state as a declaratory act of free men

1656 May 23 marks the first appearance of a woman on an English stage: Mrs. Coleman in William Davenant's The Siege of Rhodes

1660 Charles II returns to the throne, marking the beginning of the Restoration period in England

1550 – 1750

"All the world's a stage"

No era has loved theater more than the European baroque. The spectacles on the stages of the 17th century seemed both the perfect image and the symbol of a brilliant world, shadowed by the knowledge of its transitoriness.

Great social changes—the decline of feudalism and the rise of mercantile absolutism—shook the Renaissance belief in the rationality and governability of the world. The decline or reversal of traditional values increased the general consciousness of appearance and deception.

William Shakespeare was by no means alone in his obsessive comparison of the entire world with a stage in which every person has an assigned role. In the dramas of Pedro Calderón de la Barca, God appears as both the director and the observer of human life—a life that reveals itself as an empty dream in the face of the eternal truth (his most famous play is La vida es sueño— Life is a dream).

All of baroque culture seemed to reflect this understanding, and the result was brilliant theater. The 17th century witnessed the triumphant procession of opera from Italy into the whole of Europe. Architects, painters, and sculptors pursued their arts in the service of the ruling sovereigns.

At the court of Louis XIV, the archetype of all absolute princes, even daily life from the morning toilette to the evening prayer resembled a theatrical production. The other European courts competed with the Sun King in ever grander, more expensive, and more brilliant festivities. In court events lasting several days, even the innumerable banquet courses were presented with theatricality, while endless series of fireworks, ballets, and knightly tournaments framed the monumentally decorative theater performances.

In such an atmosphere, the hunger for new dramatic material was almost insatiable and provided a new class of professional dramatists with more than enough work. In Italy and England the first professional theater troupes were established; these troupes not only created and disseminated their own traditions, but also absorbed into their repertoires the theater traditions they happened to encounter as they passed through the cities and villages of countries throughout Europe. The "baroque" theater was a catchall for various theatrical genres—the ancient, the medieval, the Renaissance—a common term for the simultaneous blossoming of contradictory artistic directions. Its magic was exercised on almost all elements of the population.

1661 Louis XIV, the Sun King, assumes the throne of France

1667 John Milton, *Paradise Lost*

1672 Sir Isaac Newton invents the reflecting telescope

1685 Birth of Johann Sebastian Bach and of Georg Friederich Händel

1688 Completion of the Palace of Versailles

1689 The Declaration of Rights guarantees the English gentry a parliamentary voice and freedom of speech

1703 Foundation of St. Petersburg by Peter the Great

1550 – 1750

Journée

The great Versailles festival of 1664 spurred the other European courts to ever larger, more splendid, more expensive festivities.

Theater curtain of the Palace Theater (Ludwigsburg, Germany) mid-18th century.

1550 – 1750

Costume design for a ballet at the court of Louis XIV.

Hastily hammering together open-air public theaters with space for thousands of viewers proved quite a lucrative undertaking. At the court, the ever greater dimensions of the spectacle soon demanded the construction of specially equipped theaters. Stage technology virtually exploded, outdistancing both court theater and popular theater.

French stage architects initially imitated the Italian "peep-box" stages that separated the audience from the performing area. The perspective provided by movable scenery panels gave the illusion of depth and allowed for swift scene changes. This period also saw the intro-

Great stage and scenery designers

Inigo Jones
(1573–1652) introduced Italian stage architecture and scene decoration to England and developed it further. For the masque, he created costumes and perspectival settings that allowed seemingly magical transformations. The Stuarts (James I and II) valued him so highly that they settled his dispute with Ben Jonson over the importance of the stage designer in comparison to the dramatist in favor of Jones (1631).

Giovan Battista Aleotti
(1546–1636) invented the system for moving painted wings along grooves or rails on the stage. In this way, large painted canvas surfaces stretched over wooden frames could be pushed easily across the stage parallel to the stage front. The illusion of depth was created through painting, and this opened the way for baroque scenery changes.

Fernando Galli-Bibbiena
(1657–1743) developed asymmetrical stage perspective, "scena per angolo," for the Teatro Farnese in Parma. This angular perspective with two vanishing points eventually supplanted the monotonous central symmetry that ruled in the 17th century.

In the baroque theater, the seats with the best view of the stage were reserved for royalty. Aside from Louis XIII and his family, only Cardinal and Prime Minister Armand-Jean du Plessis de Richelieu was allowed to sit on the parquet at the Petit Bourbon.

duction of the front curtain; the opening of the curtain was meant to surprise the audience as it revealed a world of illusion. Changes of scene were carried out modestly behind closed curtains.

Europe's stage architects were constantly seeking to outdo one another. Equipment for raising and lowering the stage, wing apparatuses, installations for water and fire shows, excavations for ships and sea monsters, moving scenic prospects, clouds of strip-lighting and dimming lights—all belonged to the basic equipment of a court theater. With the introduction of tiers and loges, the auditorium mimicked hierarchical social divisions.

Sebastiano Serlio (1475–1554) composed an architectural work that had a great influence on the development of stage perspective. He described how to construct the illusion of long street passages with receding colonnades and loggias, towers and portals, with the help of painted wings set behind one another.

Ludovico Ottavio Burnacini (1636–1707) was one of the most sought-after stage architects of the early baroque. He designed the scenery for over 100 festivals and theatrical performances. His most important achievement was the design of the court pageant opera, *Il pomo d'oro*, of 1666–67.

Bernardo Buontalenti (1536–1608) designed costumes, scenery, and stage machinery for the feasts of the Medicis in Florence. His Teatro Mediceo, constructed in the Palace of the Uffizi, was the first theater to allow rapid scene changes.

Giovanni Burnacini (ca. 1600–55) built the first "Venetian" opera house with stationary wings for the court in Vienna.

Theater as spectacle

Spontaneous, vibrant, sensual—more than any other Western form of drama, the Italian *commedia dell'arte* represents pure theatrical expression. With its masks and mimicry, the commedia offered a lively counterbalance to the academic and literary theater of the time, which even Renaissance audiences found tiresome and tedious. The "art" in "commedia dell'arte" should be interpreted as suggestive of "creation" or "skill"—loosely translated, "commedia dell'arte" means "comedy of the profession." It defines the emergence of a professional class of actors, of theatrical virtuosos, who carried the commedia to its height in the baroque period.

The commedia dell'arte liberated drama from literature. Swift comic strokes combined with inventive music and choreography characterized this improvisational Italian dramatic genre—a melting pot of the various art forms out of which modern drama as an independent art form

The *Balli di Sfessania*, a series of copper engravings on the *commedia dell'arte* by **Jacques Callot** (1622), depicts the stereotypically grotesque, even animal-like figures of an impromptu comedy.

1550 – 1750

64

Italian actors at the court of King Henry IV of France.

arose. Grandparents of the young theatrical form were on one side the *commedia erudita*, a more literary counterpart, and on the other side carnival masquerades and mummery and medieval troubadours and jugglers.

The world's oldest soap opera

The commedia dell'arte was the most important form of theater of its time. For over 300 years, as the Italian troupes traveled throughout Europe, they influenced and were influenced by the various national and regional theaters. But throughout its life, the commedia retained its own distinct character: neither the archetypal themes, the configurations of plot, nor the characters changed. Not unlike contemporary soap opera, it relied on the recurrence of the same basic personality types and situations. The characters of the commedia, unlike soap opera actors, were left to their own resources to extricate themselves from their predicaments, using a rich, fixed repertoire of stage business and props for improvisation within the predetermined plot.

Characters, masks, intrigues, and "lazzi"

The seeming timelessness of the commedia rests first and foremost upon four masked figures: a miserly Venetian merchant, "Pantalone," and a babbling "Dottore"—either a lawyer or a

1550 – 1750

Life-sized Arlecchino, France, 18th century.

65

Commedia figures by Maurice Sand.

Pantalone (1550)

Arlecchino (1570)

1550 – 1750

medical doctor from Bologna—are the worthy elders who are outwitted by their servants, the plodding "Arlecchino" and the sly, quick-witted "Brighella." A fifth mask—a Spanish "Capitano"—often appears as the classic braggart. Against the masks and heavy regional dialects of these characters stands the pair of young, unmasked lovers, speaking in the finest Tuscan diction.

A typical plot revolves around the senile doctor's determination to marry the young lovers, who can only marry with the permission of the girl's money-grubbing father. The ever-hungry servants, always on the lookout for food and money, are chiefly pursuing their own ends as they help the young couple by hook or by crook to a happy end—and serve their masters with a drubbing or two along the way.

This short version of a typical *canovaccio* (prompts affixed to the walls behind the scenes) demonstrates the standard mechanisms of the impromptu comedy: conflict between young and

Lazzo of the deceptive compliment: Brighella offers to initiate Arlecchino into the language of love. Instead he teaches him only nonsense phrases and enjoys himself tremendously watching Arlecchino make a fool of himself before his beloved.

Lazzo of the menu courses: The always-starving Arlecchino is ordered by his master, Orazio, to prepare a feast for his future father-in-law, the Dottore. To pay for the arrangements, Orazio gives Arlecchino a draft for 500 ducats. He consults with Colombina about the meal, and in his excitement tears the draft into pieces to mark the seating arrangements for the feast. Recognizing what he has done, he prepares himself for a thrashing, and catches a fly meanwhile to still his hunger. After he recklessly swallows it, the fly begins to buzz loudly in his stomach, leading into an appropriate spectacle for the next scene.

old, and between rich and poor.

On the surface, the commedia seems to sympathize with the weak, but a closer look at most of the scenes reveals a moral neutrality or even indifference. The only real purpose is to ridicule whatever can be ridiculed—whether it is the decline of Venetian commerce, the narrow-minded pedantry of Bologna, or the hated Spanish overlords. Those with real power, the nobility and the clergy, are left essentially untouched. The commedia was popular among ordinary citizens, but its real patrons were found in the courts of the princes. It is therefore somewhat off the mark to see the commedia as a direct ancestor of political theater on the other side of the palace walls. Its success is to be found in its purely commercial orientation to provide a maximum of enjoyment at a minimum of intellectual expense to the audience.

The comic core of every production is the so-called *lazzi*, the clownish interludes of the servants. An "Arlecchino" has a complete repertoire of slapstick routines that he can perform on command. Along with the *canovacci*,

Capitano (1577)

Brighella (1570)

1550 – 1750

Dottore (1553)

Pantalone in distress, 20th century.

The series of scenes from a commedia dell'arte fresco on the Fools' Staircase in Traunsitz Castle in Landshut (1570) proves how respected the itinerant troupes were at European courts.

An anonymous oil painting of French figures in the commedia dell'arte of the Théâtre Royal in Paris (1670). On the left edge of the picture is the most famous student of the commedia, Jean-Baptiste Poquelin, known as Molière.

1550 – 1750

the lazzi are among the few fixed written records left by the commedia. We have these records to thank, no doubt, for modern comic figures ranging from circus clowns to Laurel and Hardy, and Abbott and Costello.

Influence on world theater

The commedia dell'arte was originally a product of both Renaissance court culture and street theater, and until its demise it swung between the two poles of vulgar burlesque and highly developed artistry. The numerous Italian troupes left their traces each year on the great European fairs; at the same time, as guests of high princes and nobles, they received the degree of honor normally due to poets and artists. Thus, the original small quartet of masks from northern Italy underwent many permutations in the course of their long journey. More than a hundred stock dramatic figures can be traced back to them—Pulcinella, Colombina, Tartaglia, Peirrot, Scaramouche, Hanswurst, Pickelhering, and Punch and Judy, among others. Aside from the

comedies, several tragedies and pastoral plays also survive that convey the tremendous power of this comic genre in their use of exotic or fantastic settings, characters, and plots.

The commedia dell'arte also exerted considerable influence on 17th- and 18th-century drama. The comedies of Molière were certainly influenced by the great French playwright's apprenticeship with the *Comédie italienne* in Paris. A century later, the Italian dramatist Carlo Goldoni created a literary memorial to the commedia dell'arte in his more than two hundred surviving plays. At the same time, his theater reforms helped rescue comedy from the banalities and tawdry burlesque to which two hundred years of devolution had brought it. Goldoni rewrote banter into dialogue, formed comic stereotypes into characters, and placed them in a social and moral context.

When Giorgio Strehler mounted a production of Goldoni's *The Servant of Two Masters* in 1947, the modern audience was given an opportunity at last to experience the comic virtuosity of the commedia dell'arte.

England: Shakespeare and the age of Elizabeth

A city run mad for the theater

In 1576, just outside the London city limits, master-carpenter and actor James Burbage (father of the first "Shakespearean" actor, Richard Burbage) opened a public playhouse which he christened "The Theatre." Burbage's theatrical experience had come in his years as a member of Lord Leicester's Men, one of the many com-

Carlo Goldoni (1707–93) was less highly regarded in his native Venice than was his literary rival, the folktale poet Carlo Gozzi (1720–1806), and emigrated to Paris in 1762. There he made theater history as the author of 222 plays, as founder of the "realistic" situation comedy, and as a theatrical reformer.

A scene from Georgio Strehler's 1947 production of Goldoni's *The Servant of Two Masters*.

1550 – 1750

The Tag-Teatro of Venice attempts an authentic reconstruction of the Italian improvisational theater, with a scene from *La pazzia di Isabella*.

Queen Elizabeth I (1533–1603) of England.

panies of players employed within the private households of the aristocracy (other such companies included Pembroke's Men, Oxford's Men, Worcester's Men, and the most long-lived of the groups, the Admiral's Men and the Chamberlain's Men—the use of the designation *men*, of course, is by no means generic!). Burbage took a calculated and shrewd risk as a businessman in building his theater, but it paid off not only for him, but for the theater of the world, as it turns out. With the Theatre, Burbage ushered in a theatrical boom unique in the history of drama. Almost every echelon of English society was caught up in the craze. Within a very few years, London saw the building of The Curtain, The Rose, The Swan, The Globe, The Fortune, and other playhouses boasting 2,000 to 3,000 places for viewers and drawing weekly audiences of up to 15,000 with their constantly changing repertoires—this in a city with barely 150,000 inhabitants in 1600!

Glossary

Arras: a tapestry hung across an opening in the rear of the stage, used, for example, by Shakespeare to suggest an additional room on the Elizabethan stage, which was otherwise essentially unornamented.

Backdrop: background curtain painted to create the illusion of depth behind the stage wings.

Passage: opening between the wings for side entrances or for placing lights.

Proscenium: the frame of the stage, designed to cover the wings, any stage machinery, and the upper stage opening (proscenium arch), could be painted with a border design to create the illusion of sky, forest, ceiling, etc.

Rake: stage floors are built on an incline called the "rake"—lower downstage (in front), higher upstage (rear) to improve the view of those sitting on the parterre.

Telari: rotating painted triangular prisms, an early form of stage wings.

Thrust: a form of open-air Elizabethan stage that is surrounded on three sides by the audience seated in galleries (the wealthier patrons) and on the ground (the "groundlings").

Wings: pairs of painted flats (canvas stretched over light wooden frames) arranged behind each other on both sides of the stage to create a perspectival stage set.

Commercial theater

This theatrical boom is chiefly indebted to the pol itics—but also to the sense for art and business—of the young queen. Elizabeth I succeeded in maintaining peace in a nation that had been torn by civil war and in making the nation into one of Europe's economic and cultural centers. Elizabeth resolutely fostered private enterprise, and many other noblemen followed her example of patronizing the many professional theater troupes that were springing up throughout England.

The goal of all the investments was to attract and entertain a broad public with money in their pockets. Drama was a user's art; no one questioned the originality of artistic performance or copyright. Whether and how often a given story was staged in London depended entirely on its ability to draw the public. As a result, authors and authorial teams searched through known materials and themes and reworked them to the tastes of their audiences.

Theater for court, theater for commoner

The Elizabethan theater effectively leveled the social classes in a manner that would have been

Richard Burbage (ca. 1567–1619), son of theater founder James Burbage, was one of the most famous actors of his time. Shakespeare, who remained a member of the Burbage troupe throughout his career, reportedly tailored his greatest tragic roles—Hamlet, Othello, Lear—to Burbage.

1550 – 1750

Toward the end of the 16th century, the Thames separated the ill-reputed South Bank from the City of London. It was in the pleasure districts of the South Bank that the Rose Theater and the Globe Theater were erected alongside the arenas for bull and bear baiting.

O! for a Muse of fire, that
would ascend
The brightest heaven of
invention;
A kingdom for a stage,
princes to act
And monarchs to behold the
swelling scene.
... But pardon, gentles all,
The flat unraised spirits that
hath dar'd
On this unworthy scaffold to
bring forth
So great an object: can this
cockpit hold
The vasty fields of France? or
may we cram
Within this wooden O the
very casques
That did affright the air at
Agincourt?
William Shakespeare,
Henry V

1550 – 1750

The new theaters resembled
inn courtyards, which had
previously served the troupes
as playhouses. The partially
roofed stage was surrounded
on three sides by the audience
which sat or stood on the
parterre and in the galleries. A
few privileged citizens even
sat on the stage itself. There
was no scenery; verbal
descriptions within the play
itself took the place of props

unthinkable in any other context. In the moment of shared enjoyment, class barriers were suspended. The pleasure-loving nobility patronized and enjoyed the theater, while the commoners took readily to this form of entertainment. While the new English troupes played regularly at courts and manors, the lords and ladies sought out the public playhouses in the London districts outside the city walls (at this time, the "city of London" encompassed but a small area of what we now think of as the British capital). Here the nobility purchased their places in "gentlemen's rooms"—loges close to the stage—for a price of 12 pence, where they were sheltered from contact with the commoners in the one-penny standing area, and the two- or three-penny seats in the galleries.

Public theaters were round wooden buildings with partially roofed inner courtyards. The flag on the roof indicated from afar what was playing: white for comedy, black for tragedy.

The performances were public festivals, comparable in atmosphere to a football game. Plays were staged in daylight, eliminating any chance to use lighting to separate the stage from the auditorium. Eating and drinking were

allowed during the performance, and for all we know, the din among the spectators may well have drowned out the play; certainly, there are recorded instances of spectators interrupting performances.

The backlash against theater

Such "frivolity" was naturally a thorn in the side of the Puritanical city fathers. The educated bourgeoisie—today the mainstay of theater audiences and patrons—were precisely those who shunned the theater in the age of Elizabeth, and moreover left no stone unturned in their opposition. As early as 1574, public performances were banned in the districts outside the city of London. The official censorship of the Master of the Revels, granted a stringent patent from the Lord Chamberlain (the chief officer of the royal household) in 1581, further constricted the theaters' autonomy.

This interior view of the Swan Theater is the only surviving contemporary drawing of an Elizabethan theater.

"Tragedy, comedy, history, pastoral ..."

The fact that the ardent blows of the censorship of the Master of the Revels could not undermine all traces of Elizabethan theater is due to the writing mania of the period's authors. Until the closure of the theaters in 1642 for the duration of the Commonwealth of Oliver Cromwell and his puritanical faction, approximately 3,000 dramas were composed to satisfy the public's immense appetite for new fodder. Playwriting became a means of making a livelihood for many a poor poet.

On average, a new play premiered every two weeks. Usually with their sights set on commercial success, the authors combined tried and true materials from traditional folk theater with elements of the new Italian classical style to create a popular mixture whereby anything that worked was legitimate. And so, in spite of the formal demands of humanistic drama, the Elizabethan theater sustained a formal complexity that undoubtedly gave it its transcendent quality. Noble and common characters appear in the same scene, the comic is juxtaposed with the tragic, and while there were those who

1550 – 1750

Costumes were always richly decorated and often cost more than a new play. The theatrical entrepreneur Philip Henslowe bought the production rights for Thomas Heywood's *A Woman Killed with Kindness* for only 6 pounds, and then invested 6 pounds and 30 shillings in the costume of the lead female role.

The Spanish Tragedie:
OR,
Hieronimo is mad againe.

The Spanish Tragedy by Thomas Kyd (1558–94) is the archetype of Elizabethan revenge tragedies. There is scholarly speculation, though no real evidence, that Kyd composed an early *Hamlet*, no longer extant, that might have been a model for Shakespeare's *Hamlet* (*The Spanish Tragedy* itself may well have influenced Shakespeare's play).

subscribed to the three unities of classical drama (most notably Ben Jonson), many authors felt free to make great leaps of time and place.

The audience, with a new kind of national pride, responded enthusiastically to historical dramas and was always appreciative of the well-placed topical or political allusion. Popular hits were the bloody revenge tragedies—notably, *The Spanish Tragedy* by Thomas Kyd, Tourneur's *Revenger's Tragedy*, and Shakespeare's own *Titus Andronicus* (and even, some might argue, *Hamlet*)—which often culminated in spectacular ghostly appearances, piles of corpses, and outbreaks of insanity.

The wars of the poets

With such irregular fare, believed many contemporaries, little literary merit was likely to be achieved. Theater, which for decency's sake had already been exiled to outside the city walls, was also considered an outcast in the temple of the Muses. Among the educated *humanistic literatti*, only the most adventurous hotheads stooped to producing drama. These new playwrights were constantly feuding and stealing each other's ideas. Brawls were the order of the day, as were sack-besotted reconciliations. Robert Greene ended up in debtors' prison;

Most of the stage directions found in texts by Shakespeare and his contemporaries have been added by subsequent editors and publishers, or constitute notes taken during performances. Elizabethan drama made sparing use of stage directions; most scholars would sooner look within the dialogue and the poetic structure for indications regarding actions, or authors' intentions, than at the stage directions. Still, in *A Winter's Tale*, Shakespeare has perhaps the most unusual stage direction in all of Elizabethan drama. Theories about the bizarre "Exit pursued by a bear" suggest a serendipitous (as opposed to a thematic) explanation: that the acting company may have come into possession of a bear and Shakespeare decided to make use of it, much the way a circus might make opportunistic use of a traveling novelty act. Whether this is true or not, it is evocative of the carnival-like atmosphere among the newly established theater world of late 16th- and early 17th-century London.

Thomas Kyd was accused of atheism and subjected to torture (and allegedly saved his own skin by passing the blame onto Christopher "Kit" Marlowe); Ben Jonson killed a man in a duel; and Marlowe himself, in a brawl marked by political intrigue and historical mystery, was stabbed to death in a bar. Still, this was an era of unparalleled theater activity, with prolific output not only from the better-known Marlowe, Shakespeare, and Jonson, but from their contemporaries Tourneur, Kyd, Beaumont and Fletcher, and Webster, and others.

The elusive Mr. Shakespeare

The biography of the universally acknowledged greatest of the dramatists is comparatively colorless. We know Shakespeare was born in 1564 to a provincial glovemaker in Stratford-upon-Avon, but the rest of his life remains relatively obscure. Church records inform us only of his christening, his marriage with the somewhat older Anne Hathaway, and of the births (and deaths) of their three children, the twins Judith and Hamnet, and their elder sister Susanna.

We have no certain knowledge of Shakespeare until 1592, by which time he was already a successful actor and poet in London. He soon rose to membership in the Lord Chamberlain's Men, and acquired partial ownership of the newly opened Globe Theatre on the south bank of the Thames in 1599. But hardly had he

Christopher Marlowe (1564–93) ranks, next to Shakespeare, as the most important Elizabethan playwright. In his first work, *Tamburlaine*, he introduced blank verse—unrhymed iambic pentameter—into the English theater, once famously referred to as "Marlowe's mightly line."

Ben Jonson (ca. 1573–1637), the most highly educated author of the period, argued publically for the use of classical dramatic rules in the Elizabethan theater. He developed the "comedy of humors," in which the striking character weaknesses of the protagonist drive the plot (e.g., *The Alchemist*). Jonson's satirical comedies *Volpone* and *Bartholomew Fair* are set in the world of London and reflect bourgeois moral standards.

1550 – 1750

Duels and fight scenes were a popular highpoint of Elizabethan show business.

The young William Shakespeare was not universally admired. Robert Greene, whose own play *Pandosto* provided Shakespeare with the plot for *The Winter's Tale*, described him in a pamphlet as "an upstart crow, beautified with our feathers, by his own conceit the only Shakescene in this country."

In his tragedies, Shakespeare analyzes—in the spirit of the Renaissance—the moral and existential composition of the individual. Edmund Kean, the celebrated Shakespearean actor of the early 19th century, made theater history with his portrayal of Othello. "To see him act is like reading Shakespeare by flashes of lightning," wrote the 19th-century poet and critic, Samuel Taylor Coleridge.

recouped his investment before he retired in 1610 to an estate in Stratford-upon-Avon where he died six years later.

This sparseness of biographical information has inspired adventurous and often fanciful speculation among Shakespearean scholars. Suggestions that Shakespeare's works were in fact written by Christopher Marlowe, or perhaps by a whole team of authors, or by Francis Bacon, or the Earl of Oxford, are hardly credited today, although the debate rages. Some contend that his works are too sophisticated for a man of such informal schooling, while others assert that his writing and his poetics are too striking, and that he was recognized by his contemporaries, such as the editors of the First Folio, John Hemminge and Henry Condell, as the most important of English dramatists.

A marriage of art and commerce

Shakespeare's plays offer an unusual combination of popular appeal and enduring literary quality. Successful in his own day, his dramas remain today the most-produced dramas in the English-speaking world (and possibly beyond), seen by more theatergoers and endured by more schoolchildren than any other plays.

Like his contemporaries, Shakespeare hesitated little to borrow from his predecessors and contemporaries if the market seemed to warrant it. To this end, Shakespeare had studied Plautus, the great model of the Italian humanists. *The Comedy of Errors* is a reworking of Plautus's *Menaechmi*, and

for *Titus Andronicus* he shamelessly pillaged the turgid tragedies of Seneca.

Like those of his less famous contemporaries, Shakespeare's history plays dramatize the lives of the great English kings from King John to Henry VIII, often using as his principal source Raphael Holinshed's *Chronicles of England, Scotland, and Ireland*. Some of his romantic comedies of mistaken identity, including *A Midsummer Night's Dream* and *As You Like It*, were apparently commissioned for specific occasions.

His tragedies, usually centering on themes of power and revenge (*Macbeth, King Lear, Hamlet*) are replete with popular Elizabethan theatrics typical of the "blood and thunder" of Elizabethan revenge tragedies—ghosts and witches, women driven insane, streams of blood, and concluding piles of dead bodies. Such devastation is interspersed with the age's stocks-in-trade—masquerades, wanton clowning, mimicry of higher social classes, and the omnipresent double entendres.

While Shakespeare's sheer theatricality no doubt kept his audiences coming back for more, his plays are further marked by his unparalleled verbal sophistication and inventiveness. The richness of his vocabulary alone, with over 15,000 words, allowed him to alternate between dour directness and fantastic metaphors, almost always within the iambic pentameter framework that served as the base for his varied metrics. But while one side of Shakespeare was happy to cash in on the popularity of dramas of vendettas and intrigues, of regicides, lovers' tragedies, and mistaken identities, Elizabethan conventions through Shakespeare's pen became transcendent vehicles for exploring human passions. Ultimately, it was their perfecting of the rampantly commercial genres of their day that allowed poets like Shakespeare, Marlowe, and Jonson to

Women were not allowed to act on the Elizabethan stage; female roles were played by men or boys. This tradition was reversed by the great 19th-century actresses who tested their mettle by playing Shakespeare's tragic heroes. In addition to Sarah Bernhardt (above), actresses such as Asta Nielsen and Adele Sandrock surprised audiences with their interpretations of the melancholy Hamlet.

1550 – 1750

Lady Macbeth portrayed in 1887 by the legendary Ellen Terry.

Lear holding the dead Cordelia in a late 19th-century production.

Ariane Mnouchkine's sensuous and exotic staging of *Henry IV*, one of the most successful international theater productions of recent decades.

give the theater of their time enduring cultural relevance.

No longer a religious ritual, the commercial theater of Elizabethan London garnered little social respect, subjected constantly to puritanical objections to pleasure. In the face of such resistance, it was incumbent upon the playwrights of the age to bolster the social standing of the theater. It is

perhaps most remarkable that we have the most beautiful dramatic writing of the Western world to thank for a thoroughly productive marriage of art and commerce.

Spain's great world theater

Theater in service to the Church

Spanish baroque theater is deeply rooted in Catholicism. The so-called *auto sacramentale*, an allegorical Corpus Christi play drawn from medieval traditions, continued to be popular into the 18th century. Spanish secular folk theater remained in the service and protection of the Church.

With the arrival in Spain of the first Italian itinerant troupes in 1535, religious brotherhoods offered their courtyards as playing areas. The sharing of the profits was a welcome source of income for the orphanages and hospitals of the brothers.

The first public theaters in Spain were modeled after these courtyard arrangements. The similarity between the Spanish "teatro de corral" and the early English theater is striking. Like the audience in the London standing rooms, the Spanish *mosqueteros*, with their loud cries of praise or disapproval, determined the success or failure of a performance. The higher-class members of society sat in reserved tiers, although in Catholic Spain, the women were seated apart from the men. By the middle of the 16th century, native theater troupes were playing throughout the land in specially built corral theaters.

LOPE DE RUEDA.

Among the pioneers of professional theater is Lope de Rueda (1505–65) who, like Shakespeare and Molière, worked as principal lead actor and playwright. He literally set the standards for the Spanish drama.

Cloak and dagger costume, 1546.

1550 – 1750

The stage was set, so to speak, for the *siglo de oro*, the golden age of Iberian dramatic culture, a popular theater greeted with enthusiasm by all classes of Spanish society.

18th-century English satiric engraver William Hogarth depicts itinerant female players in a barn. The banning of individual performances was aimed chiefly at the appearance of actresses, who had already enlivened the Spanish stage for many years.

Miguel de Cervantes Saavedra (1547–1616). Persecuted by the Inquisition and implicated in a murder trial, the author of *Don Quixote* wrote approximately 30 plays (the engraving at right, *Fighting the Windmills*, is by Gustave Doré). In the foreword to a collection of one-act interludes, Cervantes did obeisance before his great contemporary: "I laid aside my quill and Comedies and on the stage appeared that monster of Nature, the great Lope de Vega, and made himself the ruler of the Kingdom of Comedy."

With cloak and dagger for love and honor

By the 17th century, Spain had long been in decline as a world power. Its theater, however, retained the illusion of power and a vibrant life. More than 30,000 plays are supposed to have been written during this period. Under the umbrella of the *comedia*, a number of different dramatic forms developed, among which the "comedia en capa y espada"—the cloak-and-dagger play—achieved more widespread popularity.

Lope de Vega, the king of all forms of baroque drama, defined the principles of dramatic art in his *Arte de hacer comedias en este tiempo* (The new art of writing plays). A Spanish national theater, according to de Vega's theoretical prescription, would consist of plays written in three acts, in polymetric verse, using a combination of plots and subplots, about upper- and lower-class characters, and they should be entertaining. (Contrast this with the serious intent and rigid structures suggested by the neo-classical dramatists who misinterpreted

---

Genres of the Spanish baroque theater

Autos sacramentales: single-act allegorical Corpus Christi plays, interspersed with comic scenes; *autos sacramentales* were performed in honor of the consecrated sacrament.

Burlescas: farces and persiflages.

Comedias en capa y espada: cloak-and-dagger plays depicting the life of the cavaliers and nobility.

Comedias de figurón: predecessors of the comedy of character.

Comedias de santos: legends of the saints and tragedies about martyrs.

Comedias del teatro: elaborately staged historical dramas dealing (in contrast to the cloak-and-dagger plays) with the public life of the princes.

Entremeses: one-act farcical interludes for festivals.

Fiestas: courtly theater festivals with dance and music.

Aristotle and adhered to what they thought were his rules of three unities governing drama.) In practice, a typical plot involves the private life of the upper classes (the genre is named after the nobleman's ever-present cloak).

The cloak, symbol of disguise, is essential to the requisite love intrigue—usually an obstacle to a marriage. The gallant lover falls inevitably into conflict with his word of honor, which he then seeks to defend with his sword.

Lope de Vega was aware of Aristotelian poetics, but preferred the applause of the public to the nod of the pedants, and he knew well that popularity depended less on an emotional, as on an exciting, adventurous plot. In these cloak-and-dagger swash-bucklers the dramatic actions of the main characters are parodied by their servants. The figure of the "Gracioso" is reminiscent of the Italian "Arlecchino" and similarly represents the views of the common people. Naturalistic plots are as unheard of in the Spanish baroque as are psychologically realistic characters. Above all, it is a theater of allegory and parable aimed at re-creating worldly and heavenly order.

Similarly, the many works of court poet Pedro Calderón de la Barca, who stood at the center of the second great school of Spanish baroque literature, reflect the prevailing religious conviction of the vanity and transcience of earthly events. Calderón reaches his poetic peak in the fairy tale, *La vida es sueño* (Life is a dream), about the pure and noble captive Prince Sigismund, who must recognize that life is nothing more than an illusion and that all earthly effort is vain before he can grow into a just king.

Lope de Vega (1562–1635) served for many years in the Spanish navy and witnessed the sinking of the *Armada* in 1588. In 1613 he was ordained a priest and in 1627 became a monk. From his pen flowed 1,500 *comedias*, of which 470 survive. His *Fuente ovejuna* ("The Burning Village") is the only work of the age in which the peasants revolt against the tyrannical nobles.

Tirso de Molina (ca. 1584–1648) attacked the clergy, the court, and the nobility, although he himself was a monk. The majority of his 300–400 plays fell victim to the Inquisition because of their loose moral vision. Molina composed the first dramatic version of the Don Juan legend.

1550 – 1750

Pedro Calderón de la Barca (ca. 1600–81). The noble Jesuit student broke off his theological studies in favor of playwriting. In 1635 he was appointed head of the court theater Buen Retiro; in 1651 he was consecrated as a priest.

France: Classical tragedy, comedy of character

Louis XIV preferred to appear in ballets. At right, he is dressed as Apollo.

The court of Louis XIV

In France, the two great, almost contradictory, directions of European baroque theater—the spectacular courtly festival and the "classical" drama—were both cultivated. The splendor of the court of Louis XIV dazzled all of Europe. In the *ballet du cour*, a theatrical display peculiar to the French court, the king himself appeared in the midst of his lords and ladies. In the famous *Ballet de la nuit*, Louis actually enacted the queen of the stars.

The French *tragédie classique* marks one of the high points of the epoch. Under the vigilance of Cardinal Richelieu, and his Académie Française, drama had to conform strictly to classical Aristotelian principles.

The Hôtel de Bourgogne is one of the oldest theaters still active in modern Europe. In 1548, the Brothers of the Passion built a hall for the performance of farces and mystery plays. Because the Brothers held the sole theatrical franchise for Paris, the Hôtel de Bourgogne became the most important guest playhouse for the numerous itinerant troupes of the 17th century. Until the foundation of the Comédie Française, the Hôtel was the favorite playhouse of the *Comédiens du roi* and the *Troupe royale*. Later the Hôtel served as a theater for the French commedia dell'arte, the comédie italienne, and others.

Corneille

Le Cid, first staged in 1637 in Paris, by the lawyer Pierre Corneille, faced the wrath of the Académie. This tragicomedy of a fatal conflict between love and honor was deemed irredeemably offensive to entrenched standards of both realism and morality. Once a member of a five-author committee under Richelieu's authority, Corneille wrote *Le Cid* after Richelieu had terminated his position and he had returned to his native city of Rouen. But while the old academicians censured, the audiences of young people turned le Cid into a French national hero.

Corneille was shaken by the controversy surrounding *Le Cid*, though he apparently accepted the criticism, and for the duration of his career wrote more "stylistically pure" tragedies. He created the archetype of the exalted tragic hero who is above human weaknesses, a paragon of French baroque ideals—*honnêteté* (honor) and *bienséance* (decorum). Corneille's virtuous heroes tended to lack individualizing qualities. His plays were intended primarily to garner public admiration, and his characters appear more like walking templates than human beings.

Pierre Corneille (1606–84). The first great French tragedian did not consider the classical rules dogma. *Le Cid* is a tragicomedy, ignores the *three unities*, and in the character of *Le menteur* (the Liar), raises the social class of comic characters. His works belonged to the repertoire of all the leading troupes of the French baroque, but when his star began to dim in the 1670s in favor of the younger Racine, Corneille turned his back on the theater.

1550 – 1750

Corneille's *Sertorius* at the *Comédie Française* (18th-century watercolor).

Racine

A change of taste was coming. The former theology student Jean Baptiste Racine won public acclaim with his finely defined characters. His heroes are victims of their human passions, which the author subjects to deep psychological scrutiny. The rigid dramatic structure of the classical drama was complementary with his depictions of psychological intensity. Barely interested in social reality, Racine constructed his plots out of abstract dialogues that were driven only by the protagonist's psychological changes.

Phaedra, perhaps Racine's most famous drama, is a study of the destructive power of erotic passion, based on the classic myth of a woman who falls desperately in love with her husband's son. At its premier in 1677, it was a failure in comparison with a rival's more agreeable version of the same story. Embittered, Racine withdrew from the theater. Racine's elegant and musical language is generally considered difficult to translate, and like the plays of Corneille, his dramas have tended to be produced mainly in his native country and native tongue. Phaedra, however, has been a favored

role of the great theatrical prima donnas of later centuries, who hungered for strong women characters to test and display their talents. The very fact that Racine was able to write this play centered around a tragic female figure may well have to do with the presence of women in the French acting troupes. Mademoiselle du Parc, the playwright's mistress, left the company of Molière to star in Racine's next drama, *Andromaque*, about the tragic fate of the wife of Hector after the fall of Troy. Of course, Racine's

Jean Baptiste Racine (1639–99). Between 1666 and 1677, Racine composed his greatest dramas—*Andromaque, Britannicus, Bayazet, Bérénice, Iphigénie, Phèdre,* and *Mithridate*—but only one comedy, *Les Plaideurs* (The litigants). After leaving the theater, he spent his last years as court historian and reader to the king, whom he often accompanied on military campaigns and travels.

Mlle. Dumesnile, here in the role of Phaedra, was reputed as mistress of dramatic pathos. She could be touching one moment, and in the next could frighten the audience in the front rows with an angry outburst. She was known for modulating her stage rhetoric, interrupting passionate-pathetic parts occasionally with natural speech.

1550 – 1750

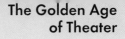

Les Fourberies de Scapin (The tricks of Scapin) by Molière in an 18th-century production by the Comédie Française.

1550 – 1750

instigation of the defection of Molière's leading lady is generally considered only one among the many transgressions that mark Racine's reputation as ambitious, self-serving, and unpleasant.

Molière

The plays of Racine's greatest rival, Jean-Baptiste Poquelin, better known as Molière, continue to be staged around the world. Ironically, this master of the comedy of character considered tragedy the queen of the arts and despite his innate gift for comedy—as both actor and author—he tried his hand at tragedy repeatedly throughout his career. Molière had helped the younger Racine to his theater debut but their attempt to work together on the premiere of Racine's *Alexander the Great* led to serious disagreement. Racine was not amused by Molière's attempt to make Alexander more believable and more lively, while the vain court audience, who wanted to see what it thought was a reflection of its own greatness in the depiction of the tragic hero, scorned Molière's profane interpretation.

Curt Bois as Argan in Molière's *The Imaginary Invalid*.

The former colleagues hence became rivals. Racine staged a second premiere of Alexander at the Hôtel de Bourgogne, a competing theater,

Jean Baptiste Poquelin, known as **Molière**, cut short his study of law and founded in 1643, at the age of 21, the Illustre Théâtre along with his lover, the actress Madeleine Béjart. It soon became clear that the business was a financial fiasco. Molière's father, a wealthy rug maker in Paris, settled his debts, and Molière began a three-year tour with his troupe throughout France. His success in the Louvre in 1658 smoothed his way into the playhouses of Paris. At first, in alternation with the *Comédie Italienne*, he played in the Petit-Bourbon; later he moved to his own theater in the Palais Royal, and his ensemble was elevated to *La Troupe du Roi* (the king's troupe). Throughout his life, Molière enjoyed the favor of the king, but suffered from the dislike of the Church. Therefore when he died he was denied a Christian burial—he died on stage in the role of his immortal *invalide imaginaire*.

and in this version he laid the groundwork for the "high style," the style of declamatory pathos, that is the hallmark of the *tragédie classique*. In the process, Racine not only encroached on Molière's audience but also stole away Mademoiselle du Parc, Molière's female lead and the greatest draw of his troupe.

But even this tragic flop could not long detract from Molière's popularity. With his first production before the king in *Le Docteur amoreux* (The doctor in love, 1658), Molière was able to make good his failure. Until his death, he remained in the king's service and under his protection.

Molière composed a long series of farces, comedies of manners, and comedies of type. Following the motto, "Je prends mon bien où je le trouve" ("I take it wherever I find it"), he stole unabashedly from the

Frontispiece from an early edition of Molière's works.

Italian *commedia dell'arte*. Together with the court composer Jean-Baptiste Lully, he developed the *comédie-ballet*, a genre in which dance scenes serve not merely as decorative accent, but as an integral part of the plot.

Molière's greatest achievements, of course, were his comedies of character. The comic effect of this genre derives neither from some complicated intrigue (as in a situation comedy) nor in the joke of a static comic type, but in the satirical depiction of certain quirks of personality, rendered *ad absurdum*. In many of these plays, the format is already suggested in the title, such as *The Miser, The Imaginary Invalid*, and *The Misanthrope*.

A cool observer of his contemporaries, Molière considered the stage a theatrical pillory, as it were, in which transgressions against reason and custom were to be unmasked and publicly ridiculed. His satirical wit targeted universal human weaknesses as well as fashionable bad habits. He satirized the burghers and nobles—how often he hit the nail on the head is evident in the reactions of the derided targets. *Les Précieuses ridicules*, with its caricatures of the fashionable aristocratic salons, brought out a few insulted marquises who literally attacked with their fists. Although *Tartuffe* clearly attacks hypocrisy not religiosity, it was not allowed to be shown for five years, and *Don Juan* was dropped immediately after the first performance and remained banned during Molière's lifetime. Molière's plays, however, unlike those of Corneille and of his rival Racine, have endured the test of both time and universality.

Molière as Sganarelle.

Branco Samarovski in a 1983 production of *The Imaginary Invalid*, in Bochum, Germany, directed by Claus Peymann.

1550 – 1750

Sarah Bernhardt as Phaedra.

In 1611, an Englishman reported back to his amazed countrymen that he had witnessed a curiosity—women playing on stage, and he found their gestures and charm so excellent that no man could have outdone them. The man's amazement is hardly surprising: although dramatic literature is full of strong female characters, from the days of classical Greek theater, female roles had almost always been played by men and boys.

In Athenian democracy, theater, like all state affairs, was purely a man's affair. While tragic male protagonists enjoyed high social standing, women, as minors, were relegated to their domestic rounds. Even the seating allotted for them in the audience was indicative of low social rank—the female members of the audience were consigned to the highest rows, between the foreigners and the slaves.

Roman theater, ever oriented toward pleasure, could scarcely avoid female players. They played no roles in any classical performances, but appeared regularly in the bawdy mime, often with no clothes. It would be inaccurate to say that women were "allowed" to appear on the Roman stage: the first actresses of the Western world did not tread the boards willingly. The most beautiful "actresses" were bound under lifelong unbreakable contract to the theater, and were often forced not only to appear naked on stage, but to engage in sexual intercourse as well.

The 6th-century Byzantine Empress Theodora, herself a former actress, granted female mimes of the late classical period the right to end their contracts upon appeal to the Christian religion, but though the Church stepped forth here as the actresses' protector, it quickly proved to be the deadly enemy of the secular theater, and of female stage activity in particular. After all, women, who bore the lion's share of guilt for original sin, wanted nothing better than to lead man astray by their looks—so argued Church Fathers—and therefore every avenue of public influence should be denied to them. The religious theater of the Middle Ages, from the earliest liturgical plays to the extravagantly bloody mystery plays, was exclusively a male domain.

It was the Renaissance, with its more worldly orientation, that finally brought change. The European nobles, especially in Italy, shed the Church restraints on modes of pleasure, just as the power of the Church was being shaken by modern science, philosophy, and economics. Although the clergy continued to preach against the immorality of the acting profession, the Church could prevent neither the secularization of the theater nor the appearance of comic actresses on the stage.

The daughters and wives of the wandering commedia dell'arte players were the first to surprise the public with their talents. This impromptu genre owed its success throughout Europe to the spectacular theatrical effectiveness of the players themselves. Their natural and lively improvisations, no doubt exuding sensuality, offered a refreshing alternative to the dull paper theater of the humanists. Moreover, in the commedia, the quintessence of modern masked theater, women appeared without masks. Their entrance on the stage naturally corresponded to the Renaissance concepts of reality, but was even more aligned with the business strategy of the new commercial troupes. The commedia dell'arte was the first professional theater of the modern world, and it enhanced its appeal quite consciously through the sensational appearance of actresses.

In its victorious march through Europe, the commedia smoothed the way for actresses by setting its sights first on France and Spain; in puritanical England, male players would continue to dominate the stage until the mid-17th century. In Germany, the stage would not be opened to women until the 18th century (it should be said that in Germany, as elsewhere, the theatrical profession was actually the *first* profession to be opened for women).

The actress was an independent, self-supporting woman in a time when most women lived under the protection of either a house, a family, or a cloister—or scrambled to survive as prostitutes. For the daughters of the bourgeoisie in particular, the theater offered an escape from the narrow possibilities of their lives and from the chains of housekeeping.

Eleonora Duse in *Rosmersholm*.

The life of the 18th-century actress Friederike Caroline Weissenborn may have served as inspiration for many a girl of her day. A leap from the window freed her from her tyrannical father and enabled her to join a wandering theater troupe with her lover Johann Neuber. Ten years later, in 1727, the now properly married Mrs. Neuber took over the directorship of her own troupe and began, along with the scholar Johann Christoph Gottsched, a reform of the theater. The status of actress offered a kind of social equality and an opportunity for upward mobility that no other occupation afforded women.

The Actress Fallen into Poverty—a genre painting of the 19th century.

Women were artistic directors, like Mrs. Neuber, or handled the financial management, as did Madeleine Béjart in Molière's troupe. They could, like the great tragediennes of the Comédie Française, amass a fortune, administer it themselves, and bring complaints of breech of contract before the court. The actresses, who were usually married, shared with their husbands both public and private responsibilites—an overstepping of sexual roles that was both intellectually and socially taboo at the time.

Of course, it was precisely because the theater was not considered a very honorable profession that women were able to enter it professionally so early. Indeed, acting had to struggle for social recognition well into the 20th century. The above-mentioned Mrs. Neuber, who insisted on proper deportment among the female members of her troupe, also struggled to improve the social view of the profession of acting. Actresses in the commedia dell'arte were, after all, known for their artistic talent as well as for their beauty. The legendary Isabella Andreini, the "first sweetheart of the Compagnia dei Gelosi," was actually well educated and even received the highest literary honor of her day—she was named *poeta laureatus*.

The esteem accorded actresses grew with the importance of the roles written for them. The actresses of the French classic period thus managed to command great respect as more plays centered on female leads. Marie Desmare Champmeslé was one of the most honored actresses of the 17th century after her debut in 1670 as Hermione in Racine's *Andromaque*.

Still, while the top stars were extravagantly glorified, the no-name actresses were generally ostracized and vilified. They did not perform at the princes' courts, but traveled from village to village. They were popularly seen to be free as birds—and when they appeared, respectable village housewives carefully hung the wash out of their way. It was apparently impossible to believe that a woman who could put herself on display could live a decent life, and so actresses, unlike their male counterparts, were stamped with a reputation for promiscuity (men may well have been stamped with the same reputation, but nobody really cared). For centuries, rape constituted an occupational hazard of the actress. During the Renaissance, the nobles in the castles considered it their *droit de seigneur* to drag the actresses forcibly from the troupe at night, only to return them to their spouses with some belittling repartée the next morning.

"And to whom does this pretty child belong?" "To me, Ma'am!" "But it appears to me that you are not married!" "No ... but I'm from the theater."

The latter part of the 19th century was the age of the virtuoso performer. The three *grandes dames* of world theater (all of whom started in the theater at a not so grand age), the Italian Eleonora Duse (1858–1924), the French Sarah Bernhardt (1844–1923), and the English Ellen Terry (1847–1928), all of an age, set a standard for actresses of subsequent eras to follow.

Isabella Andreini (1562–1604)

Each of these actresses saw the others perform. Each sought roles with similar bite and stature, even if it meant playing a male character such as Hamlet (a role always envied by actresses and vastly preferred over the somewhat incomprehensible Ophelia). Each was sought by contemporary playwrights—Ibsen, Dumas, Shaw, Strindberg—as well as by those leading male actors who were not afraid of being upstaged (Terry had a long collaboration with the English actor-manager Henry Irving). Each toured throughout the world, bringing classical, "great" drama to regions that had never seen anything more than melodrama or local revues. Each performed from childhood until the end of their lives (Bernhardt continued to perform even after one of her legs had been amputated, using various props to help her stand on stage). Each lived an unconventional life, and each commanded respect and authority.

The theater was not a friendly place for women, and the 19th century, despite the remarkable achievements of the great actresses, was not an easy time. Acting may have become fashionable, but the sexual exploitation of actresses—the careers of the *grandes dames* notwithstanding—only increased (and who is to say, in fact, that Terry, and La Duse and the Divine Sarah weren't just as subject to such mores as any of their lesser-known sisters?). An army of unemployed actors competed aggressively for scarce engagements. Now an actress, in addition to beauty and talent, also had to possess her own costumes, since these were not provided by the theaters. At a time when historical costumes were scorned as curiosities, the stage served as the model-

"Meat Inspection by the Theater Agent," French caricature, 1899.

ing runway for the newest trends in haute couture. The actress's pitifully small wages left her with little option but to spend her free moments sewing new costumes. She had two options to pay for the costly materials—hunger or prostitution. The theater management, whose invariable solution to an actress's pregnancy was to fire her, took great interest in actresses' personal lives. The sexual lives of actresses fueled the wild imaginations of the puritanical men of the 19th century. An actress known for her love affairs

Until into the 20th century, it was standard for actresses to provide their own costumes. This made them into fashion trendsetters, but often led to financial ruin. Adele Sandrock hoped to block competition from other actresses for her position as resident palace actress through her remarkable costumes.

became an object of projection for all kinds of longings, and as a rule drew standing-room-only crowds.

With somewhat more cultural recognition and respect for the theater in general in the 20th century, the lot of the actress has improved in many ways. The trend toward naturalism somewhat freed the actress from the compulsion to show herself off and feed the male audience's fantasies. The actress's roles are not necessarily reducible to her physical appearance. The emerging film industry also afforded the growing numbers of working actresses opportunities for better incomes and more favorable work and contract conditions (though whether it has helped or hurt the efforts of actresses to be seen as skilled performers rather than as pretty faces and attractive bodies remains debatable).

Even today, however, the life of an actress is a life of uncertainty.

In classical Japanese theater, female roles are played by men to this day.

The quintessence of the myth of the stage goddess: Marlene Dietrich.

Normal contracts are limited to a single season or a single engagement, and the income is surprisingly modest. This reality is often eclipsed by the glamour and hype surrounding Hollywood superstars, television icons, and Broadway leading ladies, who may well command astronomical sums. But the truth is that for most committed dramatic actresses, in theater companies throughout the world, the remuneration is small, the work unpredictable, and unemployment rampant. And, while the same may often be said for actors as well, there continue to be easily twice as many roles in standard theatrical repertoires, as well as in new popular works, for men than there are for women.

1726	Jonathan Swift, *Gulliver's Travels*
1739	David Hume, *Treatise on Human Nature*
1744	Anders Celsius develops a thermometer scale based on 100 degrees
1756	Beginning of the Seven Years' War
1762	Catherine the Great ascends the throne in Russia; Jean-Jacques Rousseau, *The Social Contract*
1765	James Watt invents the steam engine
1776	Signing of the Declaration of Independence
1781	Immanuel Kant, *A Critique of Pure Reason*
1784	Flight of the first hot-air balloon in Paris
1789	July 14, the storming of the Bastille
1791	Wolfgang Amadeus Mozart, *The Magic Flute*
1797	Ludwig Tieck, *Folk Tales*
1798	Joseph Haydn, *The Creation*
1799	Death of George Washington
1804	Napoleon Bonaparte crowns himself emperor of France
1808	Ludwig van Beethoven, *Symphony No. 5*
1813	Francisco de Goya, 85 etchings, *The Disasters of War*
1815	Congress of Vienna
1830	Honoré de Balzac writes the first of the 100 novels that will comprise *La Comédie Humaine*

1730 – 1830

George Washington, commanding general of the army in the American Revolution and first president of the United States.

The age of Enlightenment

Why? This dangerous question ruled the intellectuals of the 18th century and shook traditional assumptions. Rapid advances in the sciences revolutionized human understanding of the world, and intellectual life finally emancipated itself from religious teaching. In the age of philosophy, the only god that remained was Reason. René Descartes and Baruch de Spinoza in the Netherlands; Thomas Hobbes, John Locke and David Hume in England; Voltaire and Charles de Montesquieu in France; Immanuel Kant, Johann Christoph Gottsched, and Gotthold Ephraim Lessing in Germany—these were the mental fathers of the movement known throughout Europe as the Enlightenment.

In particular, the middle class, the economically strong but politically powerless bourgeoisie, adopted the arguments of the enlightened philosophers. In place of the decadent customs and life view of the courts, the bourgeois world demanded a more rational, humane, and just social order.

Most Europeans were too involved in the daily struggle for existence to attend much to

Hungry Parisian women attack the Palace of Versailles, 1789.

David Hume (1711–76) argued an extreme empiricism—that all ideas derive from sensory perception.

Immanuel Kant (1724–1804), the founder of critical philosophy, held an opposite position from Hume, and sought a metaphysical basis for knowledge and moral standards.

revolutionary ideas. In France, driven into ruin by the wasteful expenditures of its absolute rulers, the Enlightenment was politicized and finally came to a head in the French Revolution in 1789. Only a few years after the American Revolution, the French adopted a democratic constitution and formulated universal rights.

Throughout Europe, philosophers of the Enlightenment soon dissociated themselves from the Jacobin terror. They placed themselves at the service of enlightened princes and implemented the reforms that led to "enlightened despotism." Instead of revolutions, they preached the educability of mankind—both the populace and the rulers—through reason. And the theater, the favorite form of entertainment for all, was supposed to effect this education.

1730 – 1830

Friedrich the Great of Prussia considered himself a modern ruler and invited Voltaire for a lengthy sabbatical in Potsdam.

Bourgeois tragedy

In 18th-century Europe, a new middle class was consciously redefining its public life in contrast to the pomp and splendor of life at court. In weekly newspapers, coffeehouses, and clubs, the

95

Scene from *Jeppe from Berge* by Ludvig Holberg (1684–1754), a proponent of bourgeois theater and the first director of the Danish National Stage, the Grønnegadeteater, founded in 1748.

1730 – 1830

A bourgeois theater in the Amsterdam Shouwburg, ca. 1765.

intellectual elite discussed politics, morality, and aesthetics.

To expand these elite discussions into the broad public sphere where all citizens could participate, thinkers of the Enlightenment looked to the theater. After all, the theater's national and moral character was supposed to illuminate, educate, and improve princes and ordinary citizens alike. The extant theatrical repertoire was admittedly ill-suited to the task, as the realities of everyday, middle-class life and everyday, middle-class heroes were precluded from tragic consideration. And for the converse, the elevated heroes of classical tragedy were as unsuitable as models for a virtuous middle-class order as were the ridiculous comic counterparts.

Thus, the new genre of bourgeois tragedy brought a new type of hero. Rather than being moved to higher standards of behavior through admiration of an ideal model, the public would be moved by compassion for figures who resembled themselves. "The most compassionate person is the best person—capable of all social virtues, and to all types of greatness the most

The Beggar's Opera, by John Gay, with music by Johann Christoph Pepusch, an operetta about London's criminal class, was a sensational public success. The play parodied the exaggerated pathos of Italian opera and satirized the unbearable social and political conditions of the time, much to the chagrin of leading politician Robert Walpole. Two centuries later Bertolt Brecht modernized the material (and Kurt Weill the music) in The Threepenny Opera.

inclined," argued Lessing, one of the founders of the bourgeois theater in Germany. "Whoever makes us compassionate, makes us therefore better and more virtuous; and tragedy, which does that, also does this, or it does this in order to do that."

A look back at a new lease on theater in London

The middle-class appropriation of the theater occurred first in England. London's theaters had been closed during the Puritan Commonwealth of Oliver Cromwell, which came to an end with the Restoration of Charles II to the English throne in 1660. In an attempt to establish political and social stability, by wielding some control over the growing numbers of players and writers, many of whom had a political ax to grind, Charles issued the Letters Patent, limiting the licensing of theaters to a chosen few, and hence establishing a mechanism for oblique censorship that was to dominate English theater until the middle of the 19th century.

The Restoration, nonetheless, gave rise to a burst of dramatic energy that, left unfettered, might have rivaled the creative productivity of the Elizabethan age. But it was a new kind of drama. While John Dryden strove to maintain the classical unities, and to uphold the standards of

The London public enjoyed the sentimental tragedy. Satirical etching by Thomas Rowlandson, ca. 1810.

1730 – 1830

A 1985 Berlin performance of The Triumph of Love by Pierre Carlet de Marivaux directed by Luc Bondy.

Denis Diderot (1713–84) was both an author and the publisher of the first *Encyclo-paedia*, a compilation of 18th-century knowledge and a standard reference of the French Enlightenment. Like many enlightened philosophers, Diderot had great hopes for the emancipating influence of the theater and was one of the most important theorists of bourgeois drama.

English dramatic poetry with his tragedies written in rhyming Alexandrine couplets (the best-known is *All for Love*, a bathos-filled reworking of Shakespeare's *Antony and Cleopatra*), he also experimented with hybrids of heroic tragedy and contemporary comedy, though with relatively little commercial success. His *Essay of Dramatick Poesy* (1668) debated the merits of French and English drama and expressed Dryden's standards for a neoclassical theater.

But Dryden's contemporaries had their own view of the theater's promise, and in the vitality of the Restoration theater, the *comedy of manners*

A scene from Denis Diderot's *Le Pere de Famille*.

On the body language of those being served:
"He studies the feathers on his hat, snatches at flies like a dying man, spins his hat in front of his navel like a windmill—one must do this only sparingly—and polishes his buttons with his sleeve. When he is wearing silken stockings, he swats flies dead on his calves with great propriety. His comrades he grasps by the buttons of their jackets." (Georg Christoph Lichtenberg)

On the expression of anger:
"Anger supplies all the limbs with strength. ... While the exterior, distended with blood and bile, trembles and the rolling eyes shoot lightning, the hands and teeth reveal a form of indignation, of unrest: the hands draw themselves crampedly together and the teeth snarl and grind." (Johann Jacob Engel)

On the proper positioning of the body and the fingers:
"The posture of the body must be appropriate: the arms lie close to the body at the elbow, the head turned slightly toward the partner, but not more than necessary, so that one remains three-quarters turned toward the audience. ... [The fingers are] partially bent, partially straight—anything so long as it doesn't look forced. The two middle fingers should remain together, and the little fingers fall away from them in a curve." (Johann Wolfgang von Goethe)

"Speak the speech, I pray thee, as I pronounce it to thee, tripping on the tongue." (William Shakespeare, *Hamlet*)

1730 – 1830

was born. William Congreve, perhaps the most enduring and inventive of the Restoration dramatists, took the *comedies of type* perfected by Molière to a peculiarly English height, with *The Old Bachelor* (1689), *The Double-Dealer* (1694), *Love for Love* (1695), and the ever-popular *The Way of the World* (1700). These were comedies of mistaken identities, adultery, middle-class and upper-class foibles, cynicism,

Pierre Caron de Beaumarchais' early bourgeois comedy, *The Marriage of Figaro* (1784) was banned by the censors for six years because of its antifeudal tendencies. This is a scene from a 1983 production by Johannes Schaaf at the Düsseldorf Playhouse.

David Garrick as Richard III.

and corruption, and disappointment, though not without a strong foundation of compassion for the ordinary human social animal in all its weaknesses. Much of the action is actually driven by a contest of wit, the dialogue better characterized as repartée. When the English stage was attacked for pernicious immorality by Jeremy Collier, Congreve was quick to respond, with a broader view of what constitutes morality, and

Under the title, *Attempt at a Series of Passionate Designs for Lovers of Sentimental Art and the Theater*, these copper engravings by Joseph Franz von Goetz document the interest of the bourgeois theater in the new language of gesture.

1730 – 1830

August Wilhelm Iffland, one of Germany's greatest actors of the 18th century. He began his career as the celebrated Franz Moor in the premiere of Schiller's *The Robbers*. Goethe praised his "lively power of imagination," his gift for imitation, "and his humor." In 1796 Iffland was appointed director of the Royal National Theater in Berlin, which became the leading theater of the German-speaking lands under his direction. These pencil drawings show Iffland as Marinelli in *Emilia Galotti*.

Ludwig Devrient as Franz Moor in an 1815 Berlin production of *The Robbers*.

Ludwig Devrient, here as King Lear, was a master of the strange and terrible: "The great fiery eyes, black as his rich flowing hair, in striking sympathy with his indescribably expressive mouth, could catapult from truly frightening flashes of the wildest passion into furious scorn," wrote his nephew, theater historian Eduard Devrient.

the inherent dignity of the theater.

William Wycherley rounds out the coterie of prominent Restoration dramatists, with a somewhat more satirical bite. His greatest works are *The Country Wife* (1675), a satire on sexual appetites and mores, and *The Plain Dealer* (1676), a dark reworking of Molière's *Misanthrope*.

Moving into the 18th century

Restoration tragedy rarely fared as well as did its comedy. Many stage writers opted to rework Shakespeare or others, usually with considerable revision to reflect the tastes of the times. Nonetheless, the realm of dramatic content was changing. The tragedies of George Lillo are an example of a break from traditional tragic conventions. Lillo's *The London Merchant*, also known as *The History of George Barnwell*, is one of the earliest examples of domestic tragedy, recounting the "tragedy" of an apprentice who steals from his master. It was a success throughout Europe in 1731, and its author a dominant influence on continental bourgeois theater, though Lillo's works are largely forgotten today.

Diderot and the French

In France, a new world of bourgeois experience was already evident in the subtle psychological and socially critical comedies of Pierre Carlet de Chamblain de Marivaux. However, the decisive step to bourgeois theater was taken by Denis Diderot. Diderot, as both author and philosopher, rejected classical tragedy because of what he perceived as its lack of connection to reality. Instead, Diderot argued for a new "serious genre" in which bourgeois heroes would be characterized through their social positions rather than through individual character traits.

As a practical demonstration of his dramatic theory, Diderot wrote *Le Fils naturel* (The natural son, 1757) and *Le Père de famille* (The father of the family, 1760) in prose. Previously, prose had been reserved for comedy.

Franz Schuch in the role of Hans Wurst, the crudely comic central figure of the German folk theater of the 17th and 18th centuries.

The paradox of theatrical art

In 1741, the actor David Garrick celebrated a spectacular success in London as Richard III. His breathtakingly natural acting technique in any role he undertook was accepted throughout Europe as a model for a new sympathetic and empathetic playing art.

A crucial piece of dramatic theory came, on the other hand, in Diderot's essay, "Paradoxe sur le comédien," in which he formulated a theory that remains controversial to this day, especially through its influence on the 20th-century German playwright, Bertolt Brecht. According to Diderot, the actor should use his or her artistic means consciously and with

1730 – 1830

A group of wandering players in Nuremberg prepares to present a state scene.

Friederike Caroline Neuber (1697–1760) fled from her parents' house to join a group of itinerant players. In 1727 she took over the direction of her own troupe and dedicated herself to theater reform. She died in poverty.

Johann Christoph Gottsched (1700–66). As a scholar and a writer, he complained that the theater of his age was "Nothing but bombast and ridiculous puppetry interspersed with pomp and ceremony, nothing but unrealistic love confusions, nothing but vulgar grimaces and language."

Playbill of the Neuber troupe, Leipzig 1747.

A scene with Hans Wurst and the hero, the two central figures of the "pomp and ceremony" scenes.

control, to separate himself, as it were, from his stage character (the contrast with 20th-century *method* acting is obvious). The goal of bourgeois theater, according to Diderot, was not for the audience to identify the actor with the role, but to feel sympathy for the emotions of the character. To do this, of course, required a certain intellectual distance.

The credible illusion of reality—realism and naturalness—is therefore, paradoxically, a result of great artistry. To support this illusion, Diderot recommended that his players accept the so-called fourth wall, which became a constituent element of bourgeois theater. "The actor imagines a large wall at the edge of the stage, which divides the theater. One plays as if the curtain is not drawn" (*Discours sur la poésie dramatique*).

The curtain rises on the German theater

What we ultimately think of as the bourgeois tragedy reached its apogee in Germany. The idea of theater as a school of behavior for citizens and princes, and as a moral institution for the nation, still characterizes the German theater.

The bourgeois theater came into existence considerably later in Germany than it did elsewhere in Europe, with the end of impromptu comedies and the establishment of resident troupes. The German theater lacked a central metropolis like London or Paris, and was dominated until into the 18th century by wandering troupes, in particular from England, who re-worked Elizabethan tragedies. In the hands of the first permanent German troupes, these plays mutated into bloody and bombastic histories that filled most of the repertoire. The passion of love, the sufferings of martyrs, the arbitrary will of tyrants, in addition to the farcical, the horrible, the touching, the wonderful, the crude, and in particular the bombastic, costumes and scenery were the tried and true ingredients of this genre.

The title page from Gottsched's 1730 tract on the reform of the German theater.

Inevitably, a comic counterweight, the popular favorite Hans Wurst, appeared on stage and mocked in improvised sets the pathetic gestures of the courtly heroes. This often vulgarly cursing demoralized figure became the butt of the critics who wanted a purified and morally engaged theater.

The professor and the comedienne

With the scholarly support of the literary pope Gottsched, Friederike Caroline Neuber, the argumentative director of a troupe of itinerant actors, banned Hans Wurst from the German stage in 1737 in a spectacular symbolic action. Whether she really burned a brightly clothed harlequin at the stake, as legend has it, or whether jokers in an interpolated interlude only chased the figure out of the serious play, we may never know.

Professor Johann Christoph Gottsched had argued in his many writings for a strict

Gotthold Ephraim Lessing (1729-81). After studying medicine, philosophy, and theology, Lessing worked from 1767 as dramaturge at the Hamburg National Theater, and from 1770 as the librarian in Wolfenbüttel. A key figure of German Enlightenment, his theater works still belong to the repertoire of the German stage.

A scene from a 1981 Hamburg production of Lessing's *Nathan the Wise*, with Susanne Lothar and Günter Amberger, directed by Benjamin Korn.

Lessing's *Minna von Barnhelm* (premiere 1767) is still the leading comedy in the canon of the German bourgeois national theater.

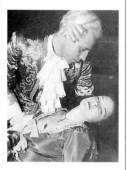

"A rose broken before the storm could tear her leaves away." Lessing's *Emilia Galotti* depicts the absolutist court as a corrupt society whose criminal energies victimize the powerless bourgeois characters. Scene from a 1942 production at Berlin's "Volksbühne."

literary diet for the theater, which, he felt, should be schooled in French classicism. Strict observance of the three unities, Gottsched felt, along with proscription of class roles in comedy and tragedy, and poetic form would offer a bourgeois theater the necessary naturalness and realism of plot and presentation.

In the educated, full-blooded comedienne Neuber, Gottsched found the ideal partner for putting his theater reforms into practice, and for finally closing the gap between between the crowd-pleasing comic theater and high-brow dramatic literature. Gottsched supplied Neuber with German translations of French classics and even provided a model tragedy of his own, *Der sterbende Cato* (The dying Cato, 1731).

Neuber, however, was too good a theatrical entrepreneur to present Gottsched's version of proper drama to a public hungry for spectacle and ardor, comedy and magic. Her preference for meeting the audience halfway (or thereabouts) led to an inevitable rift with the pedantic theorist, leaving theatrical reform—whatever that might prove to be—to be carried out by a younger colleague.

Gotthold Ephraim Lessing

In 1748 Caroline Neuber successfully produced a comedy by a young student who was to become one of Germany's most produced dramatists. *Der junge Gelehrte* (The young scholar) belongs wholly to the tradition of French comedy. Unlike Gottsched, Lessing was able to come to terms with the examples of a Diderot or a Lillo, and thereby to step beyond Gottsched's rigid demands for theater reform. In *Miss Sara Sampson* (1755), Lessing composed the first German tragedy to ignore rules of class and genre. Its success (the premiere brought the audience to tears) strengthened Lessing in his criticism of Gottsched's preference for French classicism. Imitating Shakespeare, he developed the drama according to means somehow inherent in its own context, rather than according to any externally applied poetic rules. The more enlightened Lessing undertook pieces like *Die Juden* (The Jews) or *Emilia Galotti* for a humane, liberal, and tolerant society. He understood enlightenment to be an endless pro-

cess of education, recognition, and communication between the individual person and the whole of mankind.

From "Sturm und Drang" to Weimar classic

In the last third of the 18th century, the Enlightenment gave way to the literary "Sturm und Drang" (storm and stress) movement. The movement's

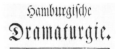

In his *Hamburg Dramaturgy*, Lessing documents his work on the Hamburg National Theater, and develops his theories of drama and acting based on empathy.

The first German National Theater was housed in Hamburg in the Goosemarket Theater from 1767 to 1769.

1730 – 1830

The Comédie Française, the earliest and most significant example of a European national theater, was founded by Louis XIV in 1680. It remains today devoted to the support of classical French theater, and is housed in the Théâtre Français, with 1,400 seats.

The Viennese Burgtheater was founded in 1741 as a court theater. In 1776, Emperor Franz Josef II designated it as the German National Theater.

1730 – 1830

mentor, Johann Gottfried Herder, offered a radical critique of the bourgeois enlightenment: single-minded dependence on reason ignores the possibility that reason can be used for evil as well as for good. The self-contained "paper culture" ignores the necessary coming to terms with human instincts and feelings. The ideals of the Enlightenment can only be realized in a culture in which both head and heart—the rational and the wonderful ("sense" and "sensibility")—work together.

The young authors of Sturm und Drang moved well beyond the Enlightenment. In *Kabale und Liebe*, Friedrich Schiller criticized not only repressive feudal conditions, but also the inner repressions of bourgeois society, such as asceticism and repression of emotions and instinct. Jakob Michael Reinhold Lenz and Heinrich Leopold Wagner, in *Der Hofmeister* and *Die Kindsmörderin*

In 1787, King Friedrich III established the Royal National Theater in Berlin. A model playhouse was built for the theater in 1801 in the Gendarme Market.

(The child murderer), presented on stage not only the oppression of the lower classes but also the dependence of the intelligentsia in service of late German feudalism. They cautiously suggest that the alternative to the misery of a utopian life lies in a free and equal society. In his work on poetics, *Anmerkungen über das Theater* (Remarks on the theater), Lenz took the "natural" Shakespeare as a model of a poet who is free from rules, who creates a new drama form through his originality. The favored genre of this period in Germany was the tragicomedy, and the favored protagonist such self-reliant heroes as Goethe's Götz von Berlichingen or Schiller's "robber," Karl Moor, who embodied the ideal human wholeness of head and heart.

The public, however, was less than enthusiastic about this new kind of theater. Goethe and Schiller, the two most prominent authors from the period of German romanticism, turned away in disappointment from the idea that the theaters could serve as an instrument of bourgeois emancipation with a direct political effect, and devoted themselves instead to the production of works based on classical models emphasizing aesthetic, rather than moral, education.

The Jacobin reign of terror following the French Revolution strengthened Goethe and Schiller in their opinion that a free society does not produce free individuals, but requires them as a condition. As members of the Sturm und Drang movement, they wanted to represent the insufficiency of nature and social misery; as classical authors, they strove to perfect an ideal of human wholeness.

Goethe, one of the first modern directors, saw the theater as a total work of art in which text,

A typical "Sturm und Drang" gesture, from Friedrich M. Klinger's drama, *The Twins*, first produced in 1776. The Sturm und Drang era owes its name to Klinger's play of the same title which contains all the motifs of the movement.

1730 – 1830

The premiere of Schiller's *The Robbers* may well have been the most successful in the history of the Sturm und Drang movement. "The theater resembled a huge madhouse, with rolling eyes, clenched fists, stamping feet, hoarse cries among the audience. Strangers fell sobbing into each others' arms, women reeled, almost fainting, to the door. It was a general release, as in chaos, out of whose mists a new creation emerged."

Schiller's three-part drama *Wallenstein* is generally regarded in his homeland as his greatest work. His highly political treatment grew from the fresh impressions of the French Revolution. As with many intellectuals, Schiller's initial enthusiasm for the citizens' revolt changed to horror at the Jacobin Reign of Terror.

1730 – 1830

In the conciliatory conclusion to *William Tell* (premiered in 1804 under Goethe's direction), Schiller gave form to the ideal of a classical harmony between enlightened princes and citizens.

A scene from Goethe's 1808 Weimar staging of Schiller's *Bride of Messina*.

narrative, scenery, movement, costume, and music must work together in a harmonious whole. He developed his own theater aesthetic and trained his players in the so-called "Weimar style." In contrast to Lessing, who concentrated on naturalness of imitation and feeling in the roles, Goethe demanded artful recitation, classical discipline, and restrained, almost static deportment from his actors, who were arranged in imposing tableaus.

The Weimar period produced literary masterpieces such as Goethe's two-part tragedy *Faust* (based on the same legend that inspired Marlowe's tragedy nearly two centuries before), but Goethe himself despaired over the provinciality

of the Court Theater at Weimar: "I was once insane enough to think it possible to establish a German theater. ... But it doesn't work ... the actors are lacking to present with spirit and life, and the public is missing to hear with sensitivity and accept." In 1817 he resigned as head of the theater when the lover of Prince Carl Augustus pushed through a guest production—in which a poodle robed as a hero desecrated the Weimar Olympia—over Goethe's protest.

Despite Goethe's disgust and despair, his contribution to theater ultimately triumphed not only in Germany but in the world's theatrical canon. With Schiller, Goethe represents the height of the German romantic drama, though both enjoyed a career that defies simplistic categori-

zation. His early dramas, *Götz von Berlichingen* and *Egmont*, show Goethe's debt to Shakespeare, though neither can quite be described as Shakespearean. The latter, the tragedy of a man whose trust in human goodness leads to his death, represents something of a distrust of the sentimental qualities he had depicted with some sympathy in earlier works, including his famous novella, *The Sufferings of Young Werther*. Of course, the *Faust* plays are Goethe's most famous dramatic accomplishment, though in fact, they have little that is theatrical in their structure and were not intended to be performed. Interestingly, in his theoretical writings, Goethe suggests that Shakespeare too is better read than performed, and this may betray some of the German author's implicit sensibility concerning the stage.

Both Goethe and Schiller readily drew upon classical models, while another German

romantic writer, Heinrich von Kleist, similarly defies rigid classification—possibly because he committed suicide at such an early age that his life's work could hardly find a direction. Kleist's work, appreciated by no one but the theatrically prescient Goethe who staged Kleist's comedy *The Broken Jug* at Weimar in 1808, has nonetheless endured, for the combination of romantic irony, sympathy, and insight with which he embued classical material such as *Amphitryon* (a classical Greek tale once interpreted by Molière) and *Penthesilea*, a striking drama of the marriage between Achilles and the queen of the Amazons. His final play, the heroic *Prince of Homburg*, is considered his theatrical masterpiece, though, alas, it only earned that reputation posthumously.

At the 1779 Weimar premiere of *Iphigenie*, Goethe himself played Orestes.

The dungeon scene from Goethe's *Faust I*.

1730 – 1830

A detail from "Goethe in the Campagna" (1786-87) by Johann Heinrich Wilhelm Tischbein.

Gustav Gründgrens and Elisabeth Flickenschild in the legendary 1957 Hamburg production of *Faust*.

1812	Napoleon invades Russia
1825	Beethoven's Symphony No. 9
1838	Samuel Morse patents the telegraph
1847	K. Marx and F. Engels, *The Communist Manifesto*
1848	Revolution in Germany (March)
1854	Richard Wagner finishes his *Ring* cycle
1856	Gustave Flaubert, *Madame Bovary*
1859	Charles Darwin, *Origin of Species*
1860	Abraham Lincoln elected president
1861	Beginning of the Civil War in the United States
1862	Victor Hugo, *Les Miserables*
1863	Lincoln's Emancipation Proclamation abolishes slavery
1864–1869	Leo Tolstoy composes *War and Peace*
1871	Giuseppe Verdi, *Aida*; Emile Zola publishes the first of his *Rougon-Macquart* novels
1872	Impressionism takes its name from Claude Monet's painting, "Impression soleil levant"
1882	Robert Koch discovers the tuberculosis bacteria
1889	Construction of the Eiffel Tower
1892	Rudolf Diesel invents the Diesel motor
1895	Wilhelm Röntgen discovers the X ray; Lumière and Méliès invent motion pictures

1800 – 1910

The romantic reaction

The political and social revolutions of the first half of the 19th century sealed the fate of feudalism and raised the middle class to the dominant political force in Europe. The third estate gained the money, thanks to capitalism, that the feudal rulers had lost.

The moneyed bourgeoisie, however, was only conditionally ready to allow the unpropertied masses (i.e., the "proletariat") to participate in their newly won political rights. The right to vote depended on taxable income, and the democratic principle of majority rule was limited by institutional correctives such as separation of powers. After the Jacobin excesses in France, fear of the mob was too strong, and the will to share the prosperity won through the exploitation of the working class was too weak to allow an easy distribution of power.

The middle class switched sides socially and now stood in the way of movements for

In the art of the German Biedermeier period, the withdrawal of the middle class into private life, and the desire for security and family life is evident. This painting shows a typical bourgeois family, ca. 1820.

emancipation and democracy. Culturally, this entailed a radical criticism of the bourgeois enlightenment, as begun by the Sturm und Drang movement.

Out of a rebellion against the enlightened adoption of culture for pedagogical and moral ends and against the submission of art to old canons grew Romanticism. The new Romanticism reflected a desire to plumb the human psyche, as experienced in folk tales, sagas, or dreams, and to seek Truth beyond the sensible limits of reason.

The Bank of England, 1894. Accompanying industrialization, capitalism established itself as the economic form of Europe.

The middle class retreat into the trivial

Romantic artists did not have a direct influence on the theater. The few works of romantic dramatists were hardly produced or were at best pre-

A German caricature of the loss of the achievements of the bourgeois revolution of 1848.

sented as readings. The treatment of current themes such as women's rights, Darwinism, the laws of heredity, atheism, and socialism was suppressed by state censors. The public, in any event, demonstrated little interest in a socially or politically engaged theater.

In Germany, localized communities erected a number of opulent theaters to show off their economic power. These commercial theaters were contracted to directors who then assumed all financial risks and ran the theaters according to strict market (supply and demand) principles. Public taste determined the program, and the theater turned away from any drama that might be too literary or challenging. In England and

Strike of English dock workers, 1889. Socialism criticized the unrestrained exploitation of workers and formed the ideological basis of the new labor movement.

1800 – 1910

The modern boulevard theater owes its name to the numerous theaters for light entertainment that opened along the boulevards of Paris in the 19th century. The plays were written for quick popular consumption and had few literary pretensions; they depended for their success on theatrical effects. The preferred themes were adultery, double morality, and mistaken identity. The favorite setting was the middle-class sitting room.

Only a few romantic dramas have had an impact on theater history. The premiere of Victor Hugo's *Hernani*, a history-cum-adventure play, provoked a memorable battle in the theater. Hugo had taken his stand against the "literary ancien régime," and overthrew the classical rules that had dominated French theater. Against the classical ideal of beauty, Hugo juxtaposed the grotesque. With the help of 300 paid supporters, Hugo managed to bring the principles of romanticism to the public.

France as well, the early 19th-century theater produced little that was new or enduring, as literature. Standard fare was melodrama, farce, reworkings of Shakespeare (including happy endings to the great tragedies), and light drama based on popular fiction.

The commercial theaters sought professionally crafted pieces that would satisfy the public's taste for sentiment, excitement, and entertainment. These *pièces bien faites* (literally, "well-made plays") traversed the borders of Europe, from the theaters of London or the boulevards of Paris, where the art of the trivial was blooming, and possibly the biggest hit of the new pleasure industry was the operetta, a light-hearted musical interspersed with ballet, after the model developed in Paris by Jacques Offenbach (not to be confused in tone with the controversial, political,

but extremely popular *Beggar's Opera* by John Gay a century earlier).

The public went to the theater for recreation, and the 19th-century audience focused its attention on the virtuoso player—the "star." The 19th century saw the rise of the cult of the star, an individual who could—albeit temporarily—bring the spectators completely under his or her sway and make everyday reality seem to disappear. No one seemed to care very much that the artistic power of the theater was subjugated to the art of the virtuoso performer, that many a leading actor hacked away at the original text to enhance his own role and suit his own fancy, relegating many a supporting ensemble to the background. (Hardly a 19th-century innovation—David Garrick had taken great liberties with Shakespearean texts throughout his career in the previous century.) Henry Irving (1838–1905) was the quintessential 19th-century star performer, and he became the first actor ever to be honored with a knighthood.

Long live the past

The romantic era in many ways longed for a past that could erase the shifting, confusing foundation of the present—a shining past discovered through empirical research and then idealized. The theater seemed well suited to reconstruct the past, literally to make the past live again.

Inspired by historical paintings, theater ensembles now began to recast their roles in historical costumes; in the Renaissance and baroque periods, stage costumes had imitated

A scene from an operetta by Jacques Offenbach (1819–80).

Eleonora Duse (1858–1924) is accounted as one of the great tragediennes of theater history. On numerous tours she carried her soulful, expressive style through Europe, the United States, and South America.

1800 – 1910

Sarah Bernhardt (1844–1923), in contrast to "the Duse," pursued a highly stylized manner of expression. This photo is from a production of 1884.

The handsome Josef Kainz (1858–1910) was celebrated by his contemporaries as Germany's greatest actor. His admirers praised the poetry and sensibility of his acting, as well the beauty of his voice: "He spoke like the wind blowing through a harp—piercing, woeful, sparkling, movingly moved."

An 1883 Comédie Française production of Victor Hugo's *Lucrèce Borgia* with historically correct Renaissance costumes.

1800 – 1910

Caricature of a conceited mime, ca. 1840.

whatever was the current dress at court. Even the demand of the Enlightenment for historically true costumes had found little acceptance from either the public or the players, who had to construct their costumes themselves.

However, under the influence of Romantic historicism, interest grew in the detailed, even painfully exact, historical environment of the plays—sometimes at the cost of the text. Charles Kean (son of the great English "star" actor, Edmund Kean), pioneer of the historical stage style in England, substituted a realistic land of Bythinium for the imaginary realm of Bohemia in Shakespeare's *A Winter's Tale*. In 1856 Kean impressed the public with a production of *A Midsummer Night's Dream* in which the

rehearsal scenes of the workers were set in an exact copy of an ancient Athenian workroom—the play program guaranteed that the furniture and tools were replicas of actual excavations at Herculaneum.

Germany's most important architect and stage-maker Karl Friedrich Schinkel, who provided numerous sets for the Royal National Theater in Berlin, proudly proclaimed the scientific character of his stage designs: scenery, he averred, "must satisfy the criteria of painters, archeologists, sculptors and architects, even natural scientists and botanists."

Karl Friedrich Schinkel's (1781–1841) Berlin 1916 design for the last scene of *The Magic Flute*.

Innovation in Meiningen

The 19th-century provincial German theater, the Court Theater of Meiningen, was the scene of an impressive theater reform development. When the art-loving Duke George II took the direction not only of the state, but of the theater as well, into his own hands upon his ascension to the throne in 1866, he offered the audience un-abridged, "unpurified" texts of the classics—by this point in the century, such fidelity to the text con-stituted a radical "departure." But, as it happened, Meiningen's previously sheltered audience managed to survive its exposure to Shakespeare's obscene jokes and bloodthirsty lust for horror, Molière's crudeness, and Heinrich von Kleist's depiction of the grotesque; indeed, they greeted the unedited dramas with great enthusiasm.

The historically correct and highly artful pro-ductions of the ensemble of George II were

Duke George II of Mei-ningen (1826–1914). The politically dethroned prince became a despot of the theater who demanded the last word in all productions. He designed his own sets for his theater and traveled to the historical locations of the original productions. In 1873 he married the actress Ellen Franz.

Scenes from Charles Kean's London productions of Shakespeare's *Henry V* (1859; left), and *The Merchant of Venice* (1858; right).

1800 – 1910

These drawings for Schiller's *Wallenstein* show that attempts were made even before Meiningen to create historically correct costumes. One of the early supporters of this new style was Karl, Count of Brühl, superintendent of the Royal Plays in Berlin (1814–28).

successful throughout Europe. With settings and costumes designed strictly according to historical research, created as much as possible from authentic materials, the productions included special effects in lighting and odors, such as gunpowder and incense, and noises such as grinding, cries, church bells, or fanfares to increase the illusion of a resurrected past.

George II was one of the forerunners of the modern theater of the director. More effectively than his predecessors, say, Goethe or Kean, Meiningen considered the entire production a single work of art in which all elements, including the actors, must conform to an overall concept. Interestingly, one of Meiningen's lasting impressions on its audiences had to do with the individuality of the crowd: extras in the Meiningen productions no longer stood around the stage as

1800 – 1910

A scene based on a sketch by Meiningen from his famous production of Shakespeare's *Julius Caesar*. Legend has it that the lead actor was selected in preference to a more talented colleague because of his resemblance to the historical Caesar.

part of the scenery, but moved, reacted, and made themselves notable, with a life of their own beyond anything offered by the text. That a popular critic rejected such crowd scenes as a "ridiculous emancipation of the masses" reveals just how revolutionary such an innovation was considered.

Players in Meiningen's ensemble, already in costume, prepare for their entrance in Schiller's *Maid of Orleans*.

Charges that the Meiningen historicism tended to overshadow the dramatic merits of the production or the literary content of the play may well seem justified in the face of the expansion to grotesque proportions of the historical stage style in the following decades. But with its emphasis on mass direction and radically realistic stages, the Meiningen theater, in a sense, was preparing the ground for naturalism.

The perfect illusion: Naturalism

Naturalism was the first artistic movement that publically addressed the suffering of the masses and social outcasts, but despite contemporary suggestions, naturalism did not grow primarily from political or social reform motives. The first concern of the naturalists was verisimilitude—the exact representation of reality.

Among his most lasting contributions to theater we must include the Duke of Meiningen's discovery of Heinrich von Kleist (1777–1811), who remained obscure during his brief lifetime, but is accounted one of Germany's greatest playwrights. Sketch by Meiningen for *Die Hermannsschlacht*, which ran for 101 performances.

1800 – 1910

A photo from the 1897 Meiningen production of *Don Juan and Faust* by Christian Dietrich Grabbe (1801–36).

117

Eleonora Duse in Henrik Ibsen's *Rosmersholm*. The play's naturalism dissected the ailing condition of bourgeois society.

Caricature of the censors of naturalistic drama, 1894.

1800 – 1910

The naturalist artist, thus, became an empirical scientist, researching the laws of human behavior. He strove in his art to create an objective, true-to-life, nonidealized portrayal of reality. In naturalist drama, the importance of the plot was replaced by an exactly detailed description of circumstance. And nowhere is reality, the naturalists quickly realized, more striking than in the physical and moral misery of urban ghettos, among the sick, the insane, the indigent, and the alcoholic, and of course among prostitutes (the best-known naturalist was not a dramatist, but a novelist, Emile Zola, whose many novels ran this very gamut of socially downtrodden and ostracized groups). While such social outcasts may evoke pity in an audience, and may inflame the audience to contest the prohibitions of the censors, they have, generally, never really started a revolution.

The first naturalistic presentations in Europe were considered scandalous. A public long accustomed to find in art either the ideals of classical beauty, or an innocuous diversion, was initially shocked by the appearance of ugly realities in what had once been the glorified temple of the muses. But naturalism had its appeal, especially in a climate of political, philosophical, scientific, and social change. A world irrevocably altered in its spirit, culture, and structure by the industrial revolution, by Charles Darwin's theory of natural selection, by Karl Marx's studies on capitalism and socialism, ultimately found in naturalist drama a reflection of the world that was believable, that was familiar, and in many ways that was challenging. Yet, the audience could watch from a safe remove beyond the theater's "fourth wall," absorbed in the illusion of real life.

Naturalism as an artistic movement focused its attention on the oppressed masses. *Weavers' Procession* (etching, 1897) by German artist **Käthe Kollwitz** was inspired by Gerhart Hauptmann's *The Weavers* (1893).

Theater clubs

Naturalism, however, in most of the countries of Europe, had to circumvent, or overcome, state censorship. Whenever a dramatist attempted to deal with current social issues, the play—if it was indeed allowed upon the stage at all—was cut beyond recognition by the authorities. The 19th-century commercial theater was anything but a forum for the discussion of immediate social questions.

A way out of this dilemma was provided by a theater afficionado employed by the Paris gas works. In 1887 André Antoine founded the Théâtre Libre, the first theater club in Europe, which became a model for the Freie Bühne in Berlin, the Independent Theatre Society in London, and the Moscow Art Theater in Russia. By playing before a closed group of members, acting troupes could evade the censor.

Antoine paved the way for modern drama, and specifically for naturalistic production techniques, on the European stage. "The milieu determines the action of the character roles, and not the reverse." Inspired by the Meiningen approach, Antoine expanded the settings to include three-dimensional objects in place of painted scenery. He used real props where possible and worked with amateur players, because he found traditional theater art too artificial. Within a few years, Antoine had established naturalism

Caricature of the naturalistic "poetry of ugliness," supposedly fostered by the Free Stage Union in Berlin.

1800 – 1910

A scene from one of the first presentations of the Théâtre Libre, *En famille*, by Méténier.

André Antoine (1858–1943) opened his own Théâtre Antoine after founding the Théâtre Libre in 1896. In 1914 he withdrew from the theater and devoted himself to the more naturalistic medium, film.

The Independent Theater Society, founded in London in 1891, wanted to revive the brackish English theater mounting productions of Ibsen. In 1892, the "first original didactic-realistic play" by George Bernard Shaw (1856–1950) was presented: *The Houses of Mr. Satorius*. Shaw knew how to combine traditional British entertainment with socially critical content, and thus ended the long reign of simple comedies and melodramas on the British stage. This photo shows a scene from a 1945 production of *Mrs. Warren's Profession*.

in France, offering premieres of Leo Tolstoy, August Strindberg, Gerhart Hauptmann, and Henrik Ibsen, among others.

Henrik Ibsen

The triumphal march of this Norwegian dramatist across the stages of Europe began in Berlin. In 1889 Otto Brahm opened his Freie Bühne, inspired by the Théâtre Libre, with a production of Ibsen's banned *Ghosts* (written in 1881, with its tale of the "sins of the fathers," which the reactionary critics interpreted as venereal disease, ignoring the metaphor for social disease that Ibsen more characteristically would have employed). In 1875 Ibsen, who had been only moderately successful in his homeland, exiled himself to Dresden where he wrote his twelve great social dramas, including *The Pillars of the Community, A Doll's House, The Wild Duck, Hedda Gabler*, and *An Enemy of the People*, which were to become models of 20th-century realistic drama.

Ibsen recast tragedy within the stifling narrowness of middle-class hominess, in a milieu where no great horrors, but rather petty outrages led to catastrophe. The central theme of many of his dramas is the deception of the frustrated average age person. Ibsen presented characters who, like the unsuccessful inventor Hjalmar Ekdal in *The Wild Duck*, can come to terms with their broken lives only through stubborn self-deception.

The structure of *The Wild Duck* is characteristic of Ibsen's entire oeuvre. A supposed friend of

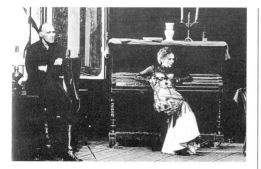

The plays of Swedish play-wright August Strindberg (1849–1912) portray bourgeois marriage as a hellish, self-destructive war, demonstrating the capitalistic struggle of "all against all" in the intimacy of family life. This photo shows a scene from a 1984 Frankfurt production of *Dance of Death*.

the family reveals little by little the history of the plot, and brings to light past failure, lies, and betrayals. It is precisely the truth that forces the catastrophe. Ekdal's daughter Hedwig, who is really the illegitimate daughter of his wife by a former lover, commits suicide in despair when Ekdal withdraws his paternal love from her. "Take away the average person's self-deception and you take away his happiness," comments the cynical Dr. Relling, probably speaking for Ibsen himself, over Ekdal's fate. Ibsen's so-called

Henrik Ibsen (1828–1906). After an apprentice-ship as an apothecary, the talented young author was appointed artistic director of the first Norwegian National Theater in Bergen in 1851, and moved in 1857 to the Norske Teatret in Oslo. He gained his fame, however, as a socially critical dramatist primarily in other countries.

social dramas were general-ly written as more person-al dramas than critics chose to con-sider (the theme of *A Doll's House*— considered by many to this day as a shocking feminist tract— is that "every-thing must be born alone"),

This theater poster of 1898 announces several dramas of the great Norwegian playwright.

1800 – 1910

The stage design by **Edvard Munch** for Ibsen's *Ghosts*, directed by Max Reinhardt at the Deutsches Theater in Berlin in 1906.

but this may be less a reflection of the critics' obtuseness than of the playwright's success at realistically placing personal drama in a social context.

August Strindberg

The Swedish August Strindberg was inspired by Zola to write in a naturalistic vein, but imbued his dramas with such a personal aesthetic vision that even Zola was baffled by Strindberg's claims as a naturalist author. His play *Miss Julie* (1888) draws on the scientific and psychological roots of naturalism, though in structure and language it attains a more symbolic quality.

Gerhart Hauptmann

The premiere performance of Gerhart Hauptmann's *Before Dawn* brought Berlin's Freie Bühne its first official theater scandal. "In the course of the play, a midwife was called for, and a doctor and journalist known for his sarcasm ... stood up waving a surgical instrument of the most discrete sort, as if he would throw it onto the stage. Raging tumult broke out," reported an eyewitness. The press, too, zealously condemned the "desolate, formless, raw hairbrained drama" with all its "obscenities."

In Hauptmann's early dramas, naturalism stepped out of the bourgeois salon and dove

1800 – 1910

In Nora of *A Doll's House*, Ibsen became an early proponent of women's rights. The play is one of today's most produced works. Scene from a 1952 Paris production.

A scene from the 1881 Chicago premiere of Ibsen's Ghosts by a Norwegian troupe.

into the living conditions of prospering peasants and hungry proletarians. Clearly influenced by the novels of Zola, his most important work, *The Weavers* (1892), depicts the historical events of the Silesian weavers' revolt of 1844, and became an overwhelming success four years after the initial scandal. The "poetry of ugliness" landed in the temple of the muses, and Hauptmann's dramas were presented around the world. Immediately after the premiere of *The Weavers*, translations appeared in Russian, Italian and Polish, while *Hanneles Himmelfahrt* even traveled as far as New York. Awarded the Nobel Prize in Literature in 1912, Hauptmann continued to produce dramas throughout his life, experimenting with genre and form, though he never again achieved the great success and promise of his earlier, naturalist works.

A scene from the 1881 Chicago premiere of Ibsen's *Ghosts* by a Norwegian troupe.

Gerhart Hauptmann (1862–1946) studied history, sculpture, and theater. From 1885 he devoted himself to writing and won the Nobel Prize for literature in 1912. With his naturalistic drama, he was even in his own lifetime one of the most often played German dramatists in other countries. His work pursues many forms from the neoromantic to the balladesque to the classical antique; his works are not often presented in Germany.

The Russians are coming

Konstantin Stanislavsky, actor, director, and theoretician, is the first Russian to take center

1800 – 1910

A scene from the Volksbühne, Berlin, 1931 production of Hauptmann's *The Weavers*.

Stanislavsky's first production for the Moscow Art Theater reveals the strong influence of Meiningen theories. A scene from *Tsar Fodor* by Leo Tolstoy, 1889

Konstantin Sergeyevich Stanislavsky (1863–1938) was theater superintendent, director, actor, and above all a teacher of acting. In 1898 he founded the Moscow Art Theater. By 1904 his concentration on naturalism and the plays of Anton Chekhov helped both to fame. In 1905 Stanislavsky turned to symbolism; between 1912 and 1920 he founded four studios for the education of actors and experimentation with a new system of acting described in his 1924 book *The Work of the Actor*.

1800 – 1910

stage in the history of theater. Impressed by Moscow performances of the Meiningen troupe, Stanislavsky founded the Moscow Art Theater in 1898. His program corresponded largely to German and French naturalism, in protest against antiquated declamatory, foolish staging conventions and settings, the cult of the star, and the entire program of the contemporary stage.

Stanislavsky attempted to imbue the naturalistic aesthetic with a scientific thoroughness then unknown to the theater arts. When staging Maksim Gorky's *Lower Depths*, Stanislavsky along with his troupe visited Moscow's flop-

houses and red-light districts in order for the actors to study the living customs of the city's poorest social strata.

Fanatical about verisimilitude, Stanislavsky demanded that everything on stage be real; even a roast goose must come hot from the oven. But his notion of the perfection of illusion was far broader than an insistence on re-creating an exact milieu on the stage. Stanislavsky demanded that actors be as true to reality as they could be, and to do this, he insisted, they must identify completely with their roles. Realistic physical action (or stage business) would occur by itself, claimed Stanislavsky, if during rehearsals the actor developed a concrete understanding of the shape of the character and his or her behavior.

In order to foster the actor's ability to imagine and portray a character, Stanislavsky developed a series of psychotechnical methods, including exercises in improvisation and concentration. He was extremely careful that his players not introduce any foreign feelings out of the blue. Supposedly universal forms of expression, such as the rolling of the eyes in scorn, led only to amateur playing. Rather, the actor should bring his or her personal experience to the role, so that every performance is played as if everything on the stage is absolutely real.

Stanislavsky's method was recapitulated and further developed by his student, Lee Strasberg, who brought his master's theories to America, where he founded the Actors Studio in New York City. The Actors Studio became the training school for many of the United States' actors, including Marlon Brando, Marilyn Monroe, and Paul Newman, among many, many others.

Stanislavsky as the Baron in an 1888 production of *The Miserly Knight* by Aleksandr Sergeyevich Pushkin.

Anton Chekhov and Maksim Gorky

Stanislavsky's role in the dissemination of modern Russian drama cannot be overestimated. His production of *The Seagull* proved that the dramas of Anton Chekhov were indeed playable. *The Seagull*, which in an earlier production at another theater was a flop, was followed at the Moscow Art Theater by Stanislavsky's premieres of *The Three Sisters*, *Uncle Vanya*, and *The Cherry Orchard*.

A scene from Anton Chekhov's *The Cherry Orchard* in a production by the Moscow Art Theater.

1800 – 1910

Stanislavsky's notion of realism, drawing on an inner understanding of the role, suited the finely tuned psychology of Chekhov's characters. Chekhov, a physician by profession, and author of hundreds of short stories, dissected with sober understatement the ailing condition—the malaise,

Anton Chekhov (1860–1904) paid his way through medical school by writing. His long struggle with lung disease (from which he died at age 44) led to the recurring question in his works of the sense of life.

the *ennui*, the fantasies, the desolation—of the dwindling upper classes. Like the majority of the naturalists, Chekhov did not set out to write social criticism, though his incisive and sceptical vision inevitably lends itself to such a reading. Chekhov's view of society is at once cool and sympathetic; he diagnoses the condition, he characterizes it, but he neither judges nor suggests a cure for it—the psychological drama courses on to its natural end.

More intentionally political and socially critical was Maksim Gorky, whose works were launched by the indomitable Stanislavsky. As a young man Gorky had traveled throughout Russia to acquaint himself with the lot of the poorest classes. His disgust at their living conditions spurred his vociferous criticism of Russian literature, which he felt preached that people needed to bear their fate. Gorky turned to the radical wing of the Russian Marxist movement and was active in both the 1905 and the 1917 revolutions. His dramas are accusations against arbitrary power and exploitation; they villify the wavering attitude of intellectuals in contrast to the self-confidence of the proletariat. In *The Lower Depths*, he presents both a milieu and a character study of the sphere of the outsider, all revolving around the question of whether one should put up

Chekhov reading his comedy *The Seagull* to the actors of the Moscow Art Theater.

1800 – 1910

The premiere of Chekhov's *Uncle Vanya* at the Moscow Art Theater in 1899.

with such conditions or fight them. His plays drew some following on idealogical grounds, but his characterizations in an age of psychological realism tended to be wooden and morally rigid.

Disturbed by the outcome of the October Revolution, Gorky exiled himself to Italy in 1921. Courted by Stalin, he returned to the Soviet Union in 1928, where he became the first president of the new Union of Soviet Writers, and the favorite son of Soviet art in the state's attempt to establish an official "socialist realism." In 1936, however, at the beginning of the Stalinist show trials and purges, Gorky applied for a visa to leave the Soviet Union. His application was denied and he died shortly thereafter.

Aleksei Maksimovich Peshkov (1868–1936) had almost no formal education and adopted the pseudonym Maksim Gorky, meaning "the bitter." Among his most influential works are *The Lower Depths* (1902), *Summer Folk* (1904), and *Vassa Zheleznova* (1910). His novel *Mother* (1907), dramatized by Brecht in 1932 as *The Mother*, is considered the first proletarian novel of postrevolutionary Russia.

The real and the anti-real

Irish-born George Bernard Shaw joined the ranks of the social realists. His early plays were considered unplayable and he met with little success until the establishment of the Royal Court Theatre, in 1904. From this time on, Shaw perfected his genius for dramatizing social and political debate, as he did in *Major Barbara*, *Saint Joan*, *Candida*, *Pygmalion*, and *Mrs. Warren's Profession*. The latter was perhaps his most scandalous (the "profession" is prostitution).

Meanwhile, Oscar Wilde wrote at the furthest possible end away from Shaw on a realist–stylistic spectrum. *The Importance of Being Earnest* (1895) strives, much like the great Restoration comedies, to be witty at all costs, to be unrealistic, or improbable at all costs, to avoid sordid reality at all costs, and so is a brilliant satire not only of Wilde's society, but of the very naturalist drama that flourished in his time.

Maksim Gorky's *The Lower Depths*, as staged by Stanislavsky at the Moscow Art Theater in 1902.

1800 – 1910

In 1895, the photography firm Lumière exhibited in the Grand Café of Paris a technical novelty that would radically and irrevocably alter the leisure and cultural life of the entire world. The first "cinematograph" was not taken seriously even by its inventor, who saw it as nothing more than an extension of photography, and at best a commercial gimmick.

The enthusiastic audiences of the first films were hardly watching "movies" in today's sense of the word, but were amazed at moving pictures of daily life: *The Breakfast of a Baby*, *Closing Time at a Factory*, and *The Arrival of a Train*, whose locomotive rushing at an angle toward the camera threw the audience into a panic.

Just as the invention of the camera could not help but have a tremendous impact on the art of painting, so the invention of the moving picture was destined to affect the theater in unimaginable ways. This technical miracle could not only represent reality more accurately than any other medium,

Georges Méliès was the first trick cinematographer in film history; he developed such techniques as double exposure and still motion.

but also offered untold possibilities to manipulate reality, while it would still appear "real." In "The Rubber Head," among many other early experiments with the new medium, magician Georges Méliès made both persons and objects mysteriously appear and disappear, or enlarged them to the point of bursting (consider what is done with special effects and computer animation today!). The remunerative potential of such a bag of tricks was not lost on commercial entrepreneurs. Such technical sensations, however, were a far cry from being at the service of art, and made their way into carnivals, circus side shows, and variety shows.

About all technically reproducible media, Bertolt Brecht said in 1932: "They are inventions that nobody has ordered" (just as today people might well remark, "Nobody ever asked us if we wanted computers!") People were not waiting for film; it arose in answer to no cultural necessity, nor as a

One of the first "moving photographs" in history: Louis and Auguste Lumière's *Closing Time at a Factory* (1895).

cult, as did the theater, music, or painting. Cinematography was a byproduct of technical progress, and without the simultaneous commercial vision of the pioneers who would go on to exploit and enlarge the new machines into the motion picture industry, film might have remained nothing but a technical and scientific toy, though it is hard to imagine that no one would ever have emerged to envision such a use of technology. The human mind, even if driven by profit motives, is an exploring organ, and prone to such inventive visions.

Film as art had to create a special public and its own artistic language. It is hardly surprising that the world of the theater, as well as the cultural scene in general, at first took little interest in the new medium. But as more and more film companies emerged, the new medium gained a toehold that would not be easily loosened, and the early film producers attempted to establish a more positive image and to capture a broader audience. The first official movie theater, a "nickleodeon," was built in Pitts-burgh in 1905. Thereafter, movie theaters were expansive, opulent edifices, supposed to ease the public's passage into the world of movies. Film programs now filled the entire evening, instead of serving as barroom amusement. Well-known authors and popular actors and actresses were drawn away from the theater in an attempt to legitimize (and popularize) the new medium, and by the early decades of the century, a "star system" was already entrenched in the fast-growing industry.

In France, the Lafitte brothers established the Compagnie des Films d'Art in 1907 for the production of so-called art films, as opposed to the vulgar entertainment films that appealed to the general public. While the first filmmakers strove to depict reality photographically, the *Film d'art* movement at first attempted to re-create theatrical reality. Actors declaimed with hyperbolic gestures in front of a stationary camera, and theatrical conventions commanded the direction, the accumulation of dramatic tension, and the style of scenery.

In 1908 *The Murder of the Duke of Guise* met with sensational success from both the public and the critics. The French *film d'art* influenced development in other

The audience room in a gaudy film house of the early years of cinema (1913). Like the legitimate theaters of the turn of the century, motion picture houses were richly decorated and offered seats for hundreds of viewers.

The Murder of the Duke of Guise.

countries. The film industry was internationally oriented from the beginning: after all, silent films suffered no linguistic barriers, and the export and import of films was considerably cheaper than going on the road with an entire live production. Films of Shakespeare became fashionable; with more than 319 more or less accurate movies of his plays, he remains today the most filmed author. The incursion into the aboriginal cultural territory of the theater caught theater owners' attention and a heated debate over the value, or lack thereof, of the cinema was launched. Ever concerned about the film's threat to the morals of the

Asta Nielsen as Hamlet (1920).

viewers, jurists, educators, and theologians were quick to join in the attack.

The so-called cinema reform movement—largely conservative representatives of the bourgeois intelligentsia—called for a "public and pedagogical battle against the filth and shame" of the cinema. Film, it was feared, would celebrate "the victory of triviality and destroy the taste of the people." It was, in short, "soulless, fantasy-suppressing pap." Theater entrepreneurs, finally stirred late to action when the cheap seats in their theaters remained empty, adopted these moral arguments to try to lure the audience back. In Germany, a stage union demanded in a formal statement that the govenment limit the growth of the cinema through taxation, the mandatory purchase of franchises, stricter fire regulations, and censorship.

Still, you can't stem a rising tide: by the second decade of this century, many players and writers diverged from the ranks of film opponents. The film industry offered new sources of income and considerably better working conditions than the competitive and unstable market of the traditional theater. Many naturalistic authors were enthusiastic about the possibilities of the new medium, invented just as stage illusionism was reaching its peak, and outdoing theatrical naturalism at its own game.

Among the early examples of an independent film aesthetic is Fritz Lang's 1926 film, *Metropolis*.

Moreover, talented people who might once have turned to theater as their chosen medium were just as strongly lured to film by their vision of its artistic potential as by an entrepreneur's promises of its profit-making ability.

Next to the cinema, the legitimate theater could no longer pretend to be the medium of choice for the presentation of reality, and it was forced to seek out new aesthetic directions. Too late, theatrical entrepreneurs recognized that their vice-grip on the popular performing arts was already broken. But it was not until well into the middle of the 20th century that films were accepted into the public canon of "legitimate"

culture. Of course, the controversy surrounding the cinema fostered a reconsideration of the new medium's qualities, and freed film from a debilitating dependence on the theater for its acting techniques, stories, sources, and storytelling techniques. The artistic language of the film was free to use cutting, montage, camera angles and movement, close-ups, pan shots, and—as the quintessential cinematic form that finally outdoes any comparable possibility in the constricted space of the live stage—the chase scene, or the action shot.

Movies that sought to do no more than somehow replicate or preserve the experience of a live theater production tended to be commercial failures. The new medium demanded new genres, just as it introduced new techniques. As a copy of the stage, wrote one French journalist, *The Murder of the Duke of Guise* only makes one long for the legitimate theater. Film must, and would, stake out its own territory.

In German Expressionist films, the relation to the theater is clear in the anti-illusionist stage sets, which are evident even in still scenes. This is a scene from the 1929 film *The Cabinet of Doctor Caligari*.

1903	First motorized flight by the Wright brothers
1911	Revolution in China
1914	Charlie Chaplin's first film
1914–18	First World War
1917	October Revolution in Russia
1920	Passage of the 19th amendment, granting women the right to vote
1921	Albert Einstein receives the Nobel Prize
1922	Benito Mussolini's march on Rome
1924	Death of Vladimir Ilyich Lenin
1927	The invention of "talkies" ends the strictly silent era of cinema
1928	Discovery of penicillin
1929	The beginning of regular television broadcasts by the BBC; crash of the New York stock market; Joseph Stalin assumes power in Russia
1931	Walt Disney makes his first animated cartoon
1933	Adolf Hitler becomes chancellor of Germany
1936–39	Spanish Civil War
1937	Pablo Picasso paints Guernica
1938	Otto Hahn: first man-made splitting of the atom
1939–45	Second World War
1945	The atom bomb dropped on Hiroshima kills 60,000

1900 – 1945

Railroads, automobiles, airplanes, telephones, and electronic data transfer have transformed the world in the late 20th century into the proverbial global village. There are no borders to prevent communication among virtually everyone. National, ethnic, and cultural differences, in some respects, have faded. We live in an age of new media. Film, television, and the computer have decisively changed the nature of entertainment for people throughout the world, and the traditional media—literature, painting, and theater—are being pushed more and more into the background. Their function as a mode of communication, their value in human development are becoming diluted, and they are increasingly relegated to the niche of an expensive luxury.

For centuries, European actors, theatrical entrepreneurs, and dramatists have struggled against the censorship of both church and state. Finally, by the early 20th century the theater, with a vast, rich cumulative history and body of works behind it, and the successes of the realist dramas, achieved the once-elusive recognition as an art form and as a legitimate force of social change.

The artistic and political avant-garde of the early 20th century wanted theater to assume an active part in creating a new culture, to correspond with the fast-changing times. But where the theater had once been the most popular form of entertainment among all social classes, a vehicle of emancipation and a status symbol of bourgeois

An early radio. Technology continues to revolutionize the means of communication and expression in the 20th century and to change the aesthetics of the older media.

society, it could no longer compete with the mass media of film and television. Theater in Great Britain, in recent years, is subject to the vagaries of the government's decisions regarding subsidies, while in New York, ticket prices on Broadway have skyrocketed, partly in response to the demand for bigger and better designs, making Broadway shows a luxury indeed. These are, of course, theatrical "centers," and to speak of their current state is not even to touch on the situation of regional or provincial theater.

Germany, which has the highest number of theaters per capita in the world, has experienced one theater crisis after another since the middle of the century: a fall in attendance in the 1960s followed by an ideological crisis in the 1970s that shook the foundations of the heavily subsidized theatrical culture. And the financial and political crises continue. Still, outside the state theaters, one can discern new impulses arising from the independent theaters that have prospered since the 1960s, returning to the original qualities of the theatrical medium. In fact, throughout the Western world, at the very least, one must seek outside the mainstream centers and theaters for the spirit and commitment of traditional theater.

Modern world utopias

In the early 20th century, economic and social changes seemed to bring the realization of democratic and socialistic societies almost within reach. Throughout Europe, the theatrical avant-garde responded with concepts and proposals that defined a new politically active position as well as a new aesthetic identity for the theater in society.

From the two movements that eventually crystalized into "art" theater and political theater, all

A great event at the turn of the century: the family gathers around the gramophone.

Film pioneer Georges Méliès in *The Rubber Head*. Film was at first only a carnival attraction; the powerful effect it would wield on society and culture was unimaginable at the time.

1900 – 1945

Television has become the entertainment form of choice in the 20th century.

the important developments of contemporary theater may be traced. For all of the differences between the desired artistic and political goals, there are a number of common points. One common premise is the decisive critique of naturalism and stage illusionism of the bourgeois theater. With its superficial stylistic and literal imitations of reality, the new wave charged, naturalism prevents deeper insight into the ever more complicated social totality. The illusionary stage, with its strict separation between stage reality and audience, reduced the interaction between the artists and the public to one-way communication.

Corresponding to new socialistic and democratic proposals, the avant-garde outlined the prospects for a new theater that would establish communication between the players and the viewers and bring about dialogue among social groups. "Public participation" in the artistic process, however, was variously defined. The courtroom plays of the Russian revolutionary theaters, for example, used role playing to train the laity in political and social transactions.

In contrast to the politicizing theater, representatives of the art theater movement strove for a completely aesthetic remodeling of

Giacomo Balla's futuristic design for Stravinsky's 1917 ballet *Fuoco d'artificio*, staged in Rome. Avant-garde stage designs of the early 20th century reflect the movement's clear rejection of naturalism.

1900 – 1945

life. With leading proponents such as Antonin Artaud or Georg Fuchs, the art theater movement sought a return to theater's primal, ritualistic roots, and wanted to create an experience of a communal rite shared by players and audience. Where the politicized theater sought social reform through dramatization of issues (and/or propaganda), the art movement strove to *embody* a different social structure.

> "The essence of dramatic art is a rhythmical movement of the human body through a space with the intention of bringing other people into the same motion, to draw them in, to intoxicate them ... And beyond this we must never forget that drama is in its very nature one with the celebrating crowd. Because drama only exists when it is experienced by the crowd—players and audience, stage and theater are in their nature not opposed to each other, but constitute a whole."
>
> Georg Fuchs, *The Stage of the Future*, 1904

The art of the theater

Before the star of the naturalist theater movement had yet faded on its own, a new generation of artists and intellectuals were already challenging its tenets. The English critic Edward Gordon Craig (son of the first lady of 19th-century English theater, Ellen Terry) and the Swiss Adolphe Appia in their theoretical writings called for a "re-theatricalization" of the theater. The art of the theater should develop independently, neither as a "handmaiden of literature" nor as a two-dimensional mirror of reality.

Oskar Schlemmer (1888–1943), painter, dancer, choreographer, stage designer, and dramatic theorist, aimed to unite dance with the fine arts. His stage design for Oskar Kokoschka and Paul Hindemith's opera *Murder, the Women's Hope* (Stuttgart, 1921) is almost—atypically for the artist—conventional.

1900 – 1945

For Appia, the actor was the living soul of the total theatrical work of art. He (or she) functioned as the mediator between temporal art, such as music and poetry, and spacial art which the actor structured with his movements.

Craig, on the other hand, considered the director the central

Dadaism protested through deliberate irrationality against the irrationality of war. Typical of dada was music made of noises, random sound-poems, and masked dancing with grotesque costumes. **George Grosz** (1893–1959) designed the figurine "Veronica the Coquette" for Ivan Goll's *Methusela*.

creative figure to which the actor, like a piece of stage scenery, must submit unconditionally (compare this with film director Alfred Hitchcock's comment that "all actors are cattle"). Craig defined the actor of the future as a completely manipulated "supermarionette" that draws its character neither from living nature nor from classical models. The art of acting was for Craig a highly disciplined and highly artificial system of body movement that expresses the "eternal essences" of strength, rest, and harmony. Craig found his models for this new dramatic aesthetic in the stylized traditions of East Asian theater.

In the right light

Appia and Craig, friends and kindred spirits, were probably the two most important influences on modern stage art. Both sought a more stylized, even symbolic theatrical design principle, to replace the stodgy, realistic *trompe-l'oeil* stage techniques. The stage is not a picture, but a space, according to the basic principle of the reformers who designed the playing space in three dimensions, threw out the detail-true naturalistic stage inventory, and brought in thick-

Edward Gordon Craig (1872–1966) was an actor, director, and stage designer. He produced plays in London, Berlin, Florence, Moscow, Copenhagen, and New York. This photo shows Craig as Cromwell in Shakespeare's *Henry VIII*.

Two stage designs by **Edward Gordon Craig** from 1904 and 1928.

lined symbolic movable pieces on a neutral universal stage. Appia and Craig also designed abstract stages interrupted by multiple playing levels and geometric forms that functioned together harmoniously.

Stage lighting, through the great technical advances of the 19th century, played an increasingly central part in theatrical design. Previously, stages had been lit, rather poorly, by candles and oil lamps. If a production required a change in ambience, hundreds of candles or lamps had to be manipulated by hand. Centrally controlled gas lighting was not introduced until 1817. Limelight (in use since 1837) and arc

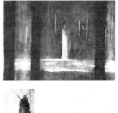

The "rhythmicized spaces" of **Adolphe Appia** (1862–1928) demonstrate his pioneering use of stage lighting.

Theater entered the modern age with a scandal. The 1896 Paris production of *Ubu Roi* by Alfred Jarry unleashed a tempest unseen in France since Hugo's *Hernani*. Alfred Jarry's audacious parody of a history play presented in the character of Père Ubu a scornful philistine uninhibitedly pandering to his pleasures and lusts. Ubu's first utterance on the stage, "Merdre!" (shit), becomes a leitmotif for the play. Jarry composed his "absurd" play as an experiment for the avant-garde theater of the 20th century. *Ubu Roi* was not only provocatively anti-naturalistic, but stood in its spectacular artificiality for a completely new aesthetic understanding. Opposite are Jarry's own program illustrations from the play's premiere.

1900 – 1945

Max Reinhardt (1873–1943) produced his theater works as a sense-intoxicating celebration intended to remove the audience from gray everyday life. He loved the theater as a "hiding place for people who had tucked their childhood secretly away in their pockets and run away with it in order to play with it until the end of their lives."

In 1901 Max Reinhardt founded his own cabaret theater, the "Schall und Rauch" (Noise and Smoke). Poster design by **Emil Orlik**.

For one of his spectacular successes, the mystery play *Miracle*, Reinhardt transformed the London Olympia Hall into a cathedral. An audience of thousands sat inside the set.

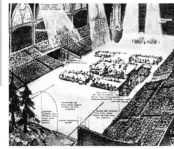

lamps (introduced in 1849) finally allowed spotlighting effects through the combination of beams. Flood lighting, depth lighting, and spot lighting have become important elements of 20th-century staging.

Craig and Appia also welcomed to their repertoire of techniques the new hydraulic machinery that allowed the stage (or sections of the stage) to be lifted or depressed and facilitated the moving of scenery (from 1882) and the revolving stage (1896).

Max Reinhardt

"What I see before me is a theater that brings joy to the people again, that lifts them out of themselves, away from life's daily troubles, into a joyful and pure air of beauty. People, I feel, have had enough of always finding their own misery in the theater and they long for brighter colors and a higher sense of life."

Max Reinhardt, Austrian actor, theater manager, and forerunner of the modern theater director, treated the theatrical production as an autonomous and complete work of art. With overflowing enthusiasm for everything concerning drama, Reinhardt left no theatrical stone unturned. He outfitted his Berlin Theater with every technical novelty—revolving stages, winding circular horizons, and modern lighting. In festival halls, gardens, churches, and plazas, he installed open theaters with arena stages for individual performances. For Reinhardt, theater was a great festival in which he wanted all social classes to participate. And to the masses that he lured to the bleachers to behold his spectacles, he offered an equal number of supernumeraries on the stage. For the performance of the mystery, *Miracle at the Olympia Hall*, in London (1912), Reinhardt used 1,800 extras, including 150 in nun's habits, a dozen knights on horseback, and a pack of hunting dogs. Reinhardt mastered the modern art of mass choreography to perfection, while employing the best actors and actresses of his day. He reintroduced ancient classic theater to the stage, revived the commedia dell'arte, and incorporated pantomime and ballet into his productions. For the stage designs, he employed artists such as the sculptor Max Kruse and the painters Lovis Corinth and Edvard Munch, as well as Edward Gordon Craig, from whom he commissioned a perfectly illusionistic stage.

Reinhardt's productions were among the largest undertakings of capitalist commercial theater history. The success of his decidedly unpolitical works, oriented as they were primarily to aesthetic pleasure, reflects the need of the public to utilize the theater as a refuge in a reality deemed ever more threatening. Around 1930, eleven Berlin stages, offering more than 10,000 seats, formed Reinhardt's theatrical empire. In 1933 the Nazis forced the Jewish theater manager, who had been working increasingly in Salzburg and Vienna, to turn his private commercial playhouses over to "the German people." Rein-hardt emigrated to the United States, where his success continued on Broadway and in Holly-wood, where he filmed Shakespeare's *A Midsum-mer Night's Dream*, with a very young Mickey Rooney playing Puck.

Reinhardt's 1905 *A Midsummer Night's Dream* was the German theater event of the year. He staged Shakespeare's most beautiful fairy tale twelve times more by 1934, and filmed it in 1935.

Reinhardt was a master of grand-scale choreography. *Miracle* in the Circus Busch (1914).

In 1924, Reinhardt staged the first German production of Luigi Pirandello's *Six Characters in Search of an Author*.

The Commissar for the People's Education, Anatoly W. Lunacharsky (1875–1933), Protector of the Revolutionary Theater, shown here with Stanislavsky and George Bernard Shaw.

Political theater

Theater has always been a political force, if not explicitly, then implicitly. It gathers people at public performances where it addresses the central issues of life. Since ancient times the reigning political conditions have been either glorified or criticized from the stage. Theater

Soviet agitprop presentation in the open air ...

history is full of anecdotes of politically motivated theater closings, prohibition of performances, and censorship. Nowhere, however, has the theater been so much at the service of the political cause as at the hands of the cultural pioneers of the Russian Revolution and of the German defenders of the "epic theater" of Erwin Piscator and Bertolt Brecht.

The Russian Revolution

In Russia, the political and theatrical avant-garde was united in their vision of the theater as an ideal medium to educate the proletarian public with a proper understanding of communism. On the periphery of the Revolution, proletarian organizations joined to form a "cultural front" and founded countless lay groups that advertised the cause of communism in the factories and on the civil war fronts.

... and in an inn: ridiculing the priest through mock prayers in the Soviet Union.

In the 1930s, over 5,000 groups with 100,000 members belonged

1900 – 1945

Proposal for the presentation of the 1920 mass spectacle *The Storming of the Winter Palace* in Leningrad Plaza.

Actor and director **Vsevolod Emilievich Meyerhold** (1874–1940) was a favorite student of Stanislavsky, although he soon turned away from his teacher's emphasis on psychology. In 1918 Meyerhold became a politkommissar of the Red Army, and in 1920 the director of the theater department in the People's Commissariat for Education. He took over the management of the Theater of the Revolution in Moscow three years later. In 1938 he was charged with "formalism" and arrested on the basis of false accusations. He died in prison in 1939.

to the amateur theater organization, "The Blue Blouses." A typical play form of the soviet amateurs was the "living newspaper" which informed of daily political events in an entertaining fashion.

The proletarian lay theater was more than a vehicle for propaganda and education. The intellectual champions of proletarian culture, the so-called *proletkult*, also looked to the effect of the plays on the actors themselves. Through participation in the theatricals, collective action and revolutionary deeds could be concretely experienced and practiced.

Such an understanding of theater is dependent on a closing of the gap between players and audience. According to the utopian ideal, drama was eventually to become a form of everyday communication. This "theatricalization" of life occurred less on a normal workday as it did on the holidays of the "red calendar." In 1920, for example, Nikolai Nikolaievich Yevreinov presented *The Storming of*

1900 – 1945

Theater October was influenced by Western symbolism. Its proponents rejected naturalism and demanded a "theater suited to the theater." Costume design for *Princess Turandot* by **Carlo Gozzi**, directed by Yevgeny Vakhtangov.

141

Aleksander Yakovlevich Tairov (1885– 1950), a defender of re-theatrization. His productions fascinated through the artistic virtuosity of the actors and the visual inspiration of cubism. Under Stalinism, Tairov was forced to return to conventional theater in the 1930s but, unlike Meyerhold, he was able to continue working until his death.

Nikolai Gogol's *Revisor*, staged by Meyerhold in Moscow in 1926.

A rehearsal for Meyerhold's Biomechanic.

the Winter Palace in Leningrad as a monumental drama employing 10,000 players. One hundred thousand spectators experienced the canonades, fanfares, overthrown tsarists, triumphant bolshevists, the attack on the palace, and the hoisting of the red Soviet flag, joining in at the end to sing the "Internationale" under the glare of fireworks in the sky.

Contemporaneous with the spectacles of the *proletkult* and the amateur productions of The Blue Blouses, Theater October, a professional theater of the avant-garde, was working on a program to systematically restructure the entire Russian theater. Under the leadership of Stanislavsky's pupil Vsevolod Emilievich Meyerhold, the Theater October sought explicitly to politicize the theater and to generate a new, revolutionary aesthetic that would share many ideals

with the concepts of the art theater movement. Naturalism, psychologizing, and stage illusionism were seen as the decadent trappings and indulgences of bourgeois culture, and the new theater would eliminate them.

In *The Unchained Theater*, actor and director Aleksander Tairov argued for the theater's emancipation from literature and revived the dramatic techniques of the commedia dell'arte. Like Tairov, Meyerhold also considered the written work as merely raw material out of which the director could fashion a drama of his own creation. He developed his own training program for his actors based on the Pavlovian thesis that every psychological condition is called forth by a certain physiological process.

This "biomechanism" was supposed to enable the player to find the appropriate bodily gestures for every psychological state; the director needed only to summon up the movements as needed.

Entry into the human paradise

After the First World War, a strong proletarian movement arose in Germany. The economic crisis that followed the failed revolution of 1919 and the Armistice inflamed the underlying social conflict. Meanwhile, the theater, fueled by promoters like Max Reinhardt, was booming. Reinhardt was drawing the public into festival halls and stadiums in droves, and theater organizations that purchased reduced-price tickets for their members could hardly meet the demand.

The young German Expressionist dramatists, influenced by the fresh experiences of the war, recognized the sign of the times and united political themes with avant-garde aesthetics. Arnolt Bronnen, Ernst Toller, Walter Hasenclever, Georg Kaiser, and Ernst Barlach protested against war and false authorities, looked critically at the preceding generation, and resisted what they saw as the repression of human personality under capitalist systems. Against decadent bourgeois culture, they backed the basic values of humanism and brotherhood, and saw the theater as an arena that would perform the "transforming deed" out of which a human paradise would arise.

With these ideals came a considerably expanded expressive repertoire. Through distorted perspectives and magical lighting effects, stage designers created a new symbolic language. Corre-

Walter Hasenclever (1890–1940). With his play, *The Son*, Hasenclever brought to the theater the Expressionistic stage set, along with the themes of the brotherhood of man and the conflict of generations. Stage design by an unknown artist (erroneously attributed to Otto Reigbert), Kiel 1919.

In 1919 the Expressionist play, *The Transformation*, by Ernst Toller (1893–1939) caused a furor. It portrayed a poet's conversion from love of country to love of mankind.

1900 – 1945

About Erwin Piscator (1893–1966), Brecht (not immodestly) commented, "I've revolutionized literature, and Piscator the theater, of this century."

Title page of a program of the Proletarian Theater.

sponding to the eruptive pathos of speech in an Expressionist drama, the players moved with a mechanical rhythm and transformed their movements into an ecstatic body language.

Erwin Piscator

The champion of the new form of political theater during the Weimar Republic was the director and theater manager Erwin Piscator. The word "art" never once appeared in his program. The stage of the Proletarian Theater, which Piscator founded in 1919, was built expressly to make politics, that is, "consciously to raise and broaden the class struggle," and to directly spur the audience to political action. His political revues, *Roter Rummel* (Red revue) and *Trotz alledem* (Nevertheless), sponsored by the German Communist Party in the early 1920s, came as close as is imaginable to this goal. Witnesses report that the huge, enthusiastic proletarian audience excited the performers and then spontaneously joined in singing the "Internationale" after the performance.

With their poster-aesthetic and agitating slogans, Piscator's revues became models for hundreds of agitprop groups that used the cabaret form to promote the revolution. At the

Stage design by **Traugott Müller** for Schiller's *The Robbers*, under the direction of Erwin Piscator.

144

same time, Piscator was managing director of Berlin's People's Stage, whose goal was to provide the workers access to the substance of a bourgeois education.

Piscator's staging of Schiller's *The Robbers*, in which one actor wore a mask of Trotsky and thus became the true revolutionary of the play, agitated so ardently for communism that it created a rift between the director and the board of the People's Stage. Founding his own Piscator

Piscator modeled the character Spiegelberg in Schiller's *The Robbers* after Leon Trotsky, using stage makeup to create a lookalike.

Stage, the dedicated Marxist recognized that agitprop theater had little or no effect on the largely bourgeois public. For the bourgeoisie, Piscator developed the concept of the "epic theater," which, unlike the emotional appeal of the Expressionist drama, would analyze and explain the complex connections between history, politics, and economics.

Projected film montage for the revue *Nevertheless*, Berlin, 1925.

To make drama into an epic at first meant nothing more than giving an epical frame to the dramatic plot. The most common "epic medium" was the use of projection. Plaques on the stage screens let down from the rigging loft showed documentary texts, film clippings, statistics, agitating slogans, as well as photographs and caricatures of historical figures. The cool objectivity of such documentary material set the tone of the entire stage—no purely decorative elements were allowed. Piscator understood elaborate stage machinery well and surprised his public with a spherical stage offering many different playing levels and projection surfaces.

Piscator worked closely with the young Bertolt Brecht, who refined and expanded the theory of

Erwin Piscator, Carola Neher, Herbert Jhering, and Bertolt Brecht working at the first Piscator stage on the Nollendorfplatz, 1927–28.

1900 – 1945

Bertolt Brecht (1898–1956). His various lovers, Elisabeth Hauptmann, Margarete Steffin, and Ruth Barlau gave up their own literary careers in order to work in Brecht's writing workshop. Brecht was known for his "relaxed" attitude toward intellectual property. **Marieluise Fleisser** (1901–74) portrayed her lover and mentor Brecht in her drama *The Deepsea Fish*, where he exploits an entire women's collective for his own success.

epic theater, though rather to the former's consternation. When the Nazis came to power, Piscator fled first to the Soviet Union and then to the United States, but returned to West Germany in the 1950s, when he attempted to reinvigorate the existing political-documentary theater.

Bertolt Brecht

"Epic theater" first mounted the stage as the creation of a great director. Piscator was conscious, however, that a production that inspired an audience to action was only halfway to being a true political theater, and he often bemoaned the sparseness of adequate literary material. In Bertolt Brecht, Piscator found *the* author for the epic drama. In contrast to naturalism, epic drama would not be content to reflect the world passively, but instead would portray it as being in need of change and capable of reform; the job of the theater was to inspire the spectators to participate in such transformation.

Brecht was convinced that only those who understood the principles of the world could change it. He compared the theater to a scientific endeavor in which the audience participates in the experiment. For Brecht, the freedom of the spectator was critical; the theater was not to proclaim and command, it was not to dole out a specific program of instruction, but

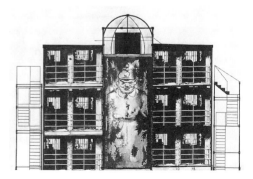

Proposal for stage scaffolding with several playing levels for Piscator's 1927 Berlin production of Ernst Toller's *Hurray! We're Alive*.

1900 – 1945

Otto Reigbert's 1922 stage design for a Munich production of Brecht's *Drums in the Night*.

was to offer the audience insight into the way of the world, and allow the audience to decide for itself how it should act.

A scene from the 1922 Munich production of *Drums in the Night*.

For Brecht, such autonomous recognition assumed a distance between the observer and the subject. If the supposedly familiar reality is in fact to be portrayed as changeable, it must be revealed in a new light and questioned. The real laws of a trusted reality are easier to discover if they can be

observed from a historical or geographical distance. Brecht, therefore, "alienated" his stories by setting them in exotic milieus or in the past. *The Good Woman of Szechuan*, the sad fable of the impossibility of remaining good in an evil world, is set in China—certainly an exotic locale—while the antiwar play *Mother Courage* takes place during the Thirty Years War.

Helene Weigel as Mother Courage in Brecht's own production of 1949.

1900 – 1945

Alienation became the central tenet in Brecht's theory of epic theater. He generated an arsenal of "alienating effects" to prevent the audience from feeling too much sympathy with the heroes or events on stage. "The viewer should not experience the events directly, but analyze them," he advised.

Stage set by **Theo Otto** for a 1963 production of *Mother Courage and her Children* in Haifa, Israel.

In his antifascist parable *The Resistible Rise of Arturo Ui*, Brecht portrayed the career of Hitler as a Chicago gangster. In this scene, from a 1959 Berlin Ensemble production, Ui is taking acting lessons to improve his public image.

The most important alienation process fell to the actor. Instead of working himself totally into the character, he should present it, but at the same time distance himself from the character's actions. Brecht's dialogues are interrupted by songs, conferences, and addresses in which the players step out of their roles and comment on the happenings, always reminding the spectator of the artificiality of the experience so that he or she will not suspend the process of reflection.

The alienation of the actor was supported by the stage design, the costumes, masks, and lighting. Brecht made free use of the projection of scene titles or film sequences to draw universal connections between events, as had Piscator. At the premiere of *Drums in the Night*, Brecht erected signs with slogans and proverbs like "It's totally normal theater," or "Don't look so romantic," even in the audience area in order to eliminate any possible "suspension of disbelief" (to borrow a phrase from Coleridge).

Brecht wrote his most important and most produced plays in exile (he first fled to Denmark to escape Nazi persecution in 1933, then to Finland, and then to the United States) between 1938 and 1945: *The Life of Galileo*, *The Good Woman of Szechuan*, *Mother Courage and her Children*, and *The Caucasian Chalk Circle*. The only audience accessible to Brecht's works in their original German during the Third Reich was in Zurich. Much to the playwright's bitter disappointment, and not without a fair twist of irony, the audience at the Zurich premiere of *Mother Courage* identified strongly with the title character—the unscrupulous war profiteer who loses everything and learns nothing. Her brave will to survive stirred the sympathy of the audience; she

1900 – 1945

"First food, then morality." The *Threepenny Opera*, with its spirited songs, made Brecht and Weill famous overnight. This is a photo from a 1979 production in Wuppertal.

Shen-Te, the good woman of Szechuan, in Giorgio Strehler's 1977 production in Hamburg.

was loved rather then judged. Alas, where was the alienation effect? After the Second World War, Brecht was offered his own theater, the Berlin Ensemble, in East Berlin where he could put his theories into practice. His productions there were fully documented to serve as the models for later performances.

For many, Brecht's greatest influence on the theater derives from his body of theory rather than through his plays themselves. His theater of alienation stands parallel in many respects alongside the "theater of cruelty" of Antonin Artaud, the French theoretician. Both Brecht and Artaud sought a theater that could have an impact—and ultimately serve a political end—on "real" life, but in diametrically opposed manners. Where Brecht wished to instruct, Artaud wished to assault, though not always with cruelty—he wished to engage the senses, to shock the audience, and to carry the action of the theater beyond the confines of the stage. Unlike Brecht, however, Artaud had little success as either an actor or a director, and he did not write plays. His major contribution to theater lay in his theoretical text, *The Theater and Its Double*. Theater of the 20th century in one way or another owes a debt to the dialectic spawned by Artaud at one extreme and Brecht at the other.

With the light gangster opera *Happy End* (music by Kurt Weill) Brecht and Weill tried to repeat their success with *The Threepenny Opera*. Although *Happy End* flopped at its 1929 Berlin premiere, it actually was a hit on Broadway in 1977. This is a scene from the 1983 Frankfurt production directed by Frank Moritz.

"The temptation to do good is a terrible thing." Brecht's *The Caucasian Chalk Circle* at the Berliner Ensemble, 1954.

1900 – 1945

"Do you want art, or something for children?" With this question, the caricaturist and children's theater playwright Friedrich K. Waechter honed in on a general antagonism against children's theater—and in the same breath dismissed the question as nonsense. But art is often considered an arena for adults only, and from this perspective, of course, children's theater is nothing but a child's toy, which must somehow have a redeeming educational function.

The idea of a theater for children, which implies that children are excluded from the cultural life of adults, is actually a fairly new phenomenon, measured against the entire history of the theater. Until into the 19th century, children simply participated in the theater life of adults, both as players and as audience. There were productions by ensembles of children in the 18th century, but these quaint and precious recapitulations of classical works and choreographical displays were not directed toward a child audience.

Putting the "little monkeys" on display, as Lessing disparagingly described child pantomimes, amused the adult world and proved highly profitable. Business-minded principals had no scruples about exploiting such an attraction. The invention of the Christmas performances is indebted to a similar marketing strategy: from the middle of the 19th century, performing fairy tales for a children's audience was intended to fill the lull in theater attendance during Advent, but the children's performances often became the hit of the season. Even today, the kitschy and usually indifferently produced (and therefore scorned by professional actors) children's programs tenaciously hold their slot in the schedules of even renowned theaters, and serve to puff up the annual average of seat utilization.

The ever-important rise of the middle class brought with it an interest in instructive children's theater. "Childhood"—the invention of an enfranchised middle class that declared the vulnerability, and hence the need for protection, of the formative years—demanded a culture for children that would be consistent with current concepts of child rearing. The first didactic plays for children, meant to teach such virtues as diligence, humility, propriety, politeness, and obedience, appeared in the age of the "theater as moral institution" in 18th-century Europe.

Natalia Saz's production of *Master Röckle* by Günther Dieke at the Moscow Gosudarstvenny Detski Music Theater.

At the turn of the century, the newly reformed pedagogy insisted that children should be kept away from the evils of reality as long as possible (an analogy to the state of innocence in the Garden of Eden, before Eve ate of the fruit of the tree of knowledge of good and evil is probably not a matter of coincidence), and should be entertained with fantasy adventures played out in a romanticized child-world. Works such as *Peter Pan* (1904) by James Barrie are still the bread and butter of children's theater.

The cultural commissars in the Soviet Union, realizing that today's children are tomorrow's adults, in the years after the Russian Revolution took a particular interest in children's theater. Natalia Saz founded the first children's theater with its own playhouse in Moscow in 1918, and there she experimented with both techniques and plays that, according to the doctrine of socialist realism, would not only explain the world but also help to change it. Special research techniques were developed to measure the reception of the new plays among test groups of children. Saz's work became a model for children's theater throughout the socialist world, where from then on children's theater attained a degree of respect that is still only dreamed of in the West. Elsewhere, children's theater was largely left to independent groups who saw in the cultivation of child audiences a seed of hope for

Until recent years, children's theater was not really taken seriously by "grownups." The musical *Line 1* won the drama prize of Mühlheim, and led the list of most played pieces in West Germany for several seasons.

the future of the theater. In an attempt to liberate children's theater from escapist sugar-plum productions, theaters such as the Grips Theater (founded in 1966) have declared war on condescension to children. In place of fiddle-playing ladybugs, author Volker Ludwig and his ensemble dramatize school problems, drug abuse, environmental issues, and insufferable janitors and parents engaged in the "class" struggle in every sense. The child-heroes of this clearly political but also enjoyable theater question the reality of the world as defined and defended by adults and through their own solidarity create a utopian society. Ludwig, whose plays have been translated into 40 languages and performed throughout the world, thinks of himself as following in the tradition of Brecht when he defines his children's theater as a "utility" with no artistic pretensions.

Socially active children's theater has served to raise the entire profile

"Rote Grütze Theater," *No One Talks About It.*

of children's theater in western Europe, and in the eyes of the ministries of culture. Theater for young people is no longer exclusively dismissed as an entertaining box-office success and is now judged on more substantial standards than the observation of "rosy cheeks" and "shining eyes" in the audience. And in the vanguard developing truly dramatic, as opposed to merely didactic, art for children stands Sweden.

In *Children Need Fairy Tales*, American child psychologist Bruno Bettelheim rehabilitated fantastic and mythic materials for children's theater. Children's theater has exchanged its political interest in the child for a sense of the vulnerability of the child who stands at the mercy of the world of adults. Recent children's theater no longer demands that children should struggle valiantly against prevailing

conditions, but sees itself as an advocate for oppressed children.

In the search for child-oriented theater and dramaturgy, experiments with new styles of writing and playing set new artistic standards. Both Swedish and German authors have influenced the children's theater of The Netherlands, from which in turn the perhaps most exciting impulses in children's theater are emerging today. The theater Wederzijds and its much imitated author Ad de Bont inspired the entire children's theater scene by stepping over the boundaries to include music, dance, and the fine arts in his productions.

Normally ignored by the general public, and only sparingly supported by subsidies, children's theater has long since transformed itself from a commercial child's diversion into a legitimate form of art. In the shadow of a glitzy popular culture, children's theater has preserved a political and

Friedrich K. Waechter considers children's theater a "school for seeing." His fairy tales and clown plays are among the most beautiful that German children's theater has to offer. *The Devil with the Three Golden Hairs* in a production by the Theater in Marienbad, Freiburg.

social engagement that is often missing from adult theater. In 1990 Ludwig's Grips Theater succeeded in bringing out a work about the fall of the Berlin Wall only a few months after the event. In 1995, de Bont's classroom theater offered *Mirad—A Boy from Bosnia*, an impressive example of how the supposedly flat medium of theater can teach both children and adults more about a war than three years' worth of journalism.

The Västanå Teater of Sweden drew its audience into the world of Nordic saga with *Den blinda drottingen* (The blind walkers).

While theater and theatrical process have been invoked in recent years in efforts to educate children, much as they had been used by the schools' drama of the late Middle Ages and early Renaissance, such programs today tend to be more open-ended and open-minded, to create situations using a more improvisational approach, rather than to inculcate principles by means of repetition and recital. But a new wave of thinking about both art and children's entertainment has inspired other contemporary groups to look back as well, and to find in ancient traditions and popular customs a new kind and a new quality of theatricality that is opening up the dimensions of what we traditionally consider the realm of children's theater.

Stripped of the grotesque side shows and abusive displays of animals, two current touring companies have combined the performing skills of the circus with the spectacular possibilities of the theater. New York's Big Apple Circus and the French-Canadian Cirque du Soleil have scoured the world for amazing and aesthetically provocative circus-type performers and choreographed their programs into thematically unified shows. The Big Apple Circus re-designs and rewrites its program each year, not only to accommodate the varying acts it hires, but to develop a new theme, such as the recent return to Coney Island—once a gay nineties seaside amusement park. Cirque du Soleil, in programs with intriguing titles such as *Saltimbanco* and *Alegria*, incorporate original rock-influenced music with commedia dell'arte style costumes and masks and manners. Hardly the exclusive province of children, these companies nonetheless elevate the nature of entertainment for children and set a new and wonderful standard, with stylization that at once looks to a mysterious future and back to a theatrically rich past.

1963	Assassination of President John F. Kennedy
1965–66	Cultural Revolution in China
1968	Prague Spring; assassination of Martin Luther King in April and Robert F. Kennedy in June
1969	Neil Armstrong becomes the first man to set foot on the moon
1974	Richard M. Nixon resigns from the presidency after the Watergate scandals threatened his impeachment
1975	The Vietnam War ends with a communist victory
1989	The Ayatollah Khomeini calls for the death of author Salman Rushdie; Chinese military ends protests in Tiananmen Square in Beijing with a bloodbath
1990	Germany reunited
1991	The Soviet Union is dissolved
1992	Outbreak of civil war in the Balkans

A 1954 Munich production of Samuel Beckett's *Waiting for Godot* with Ernst Schröder and Heinz Rühmann.

The endgame of the theater of the absurd

They've been waiting since 1953. Vladimir and Estragon, two vagabonds, sit under the remains of a tree trunk and pass the hours of their boredom with nonsensical games. But Godot, who is supposed to come and explain the meaning of life to them and rescue them from their boredom, never appears. Vladimir and Estragon remain alone together: they talk because they don't want to be silent, pretend to have feelings that they can't actually discern, ask themselves questions for which there are no answers.

The absurd clown play *Waiting for Godot* made its author Samuel Beckett famous overnight. Beckett's work expresses the forlorn state of humankind after the Second World War, when people faced the leveling not only of their homes, but also of their traditional religious and ethical bonds. The desolation of Europe, the horrors of the concentration and extermination camps at Auschwitz and Dachau

Jean-Paul Sartre (1905–80), French existentialist, composed philosophical dramas in which each person struggles to control the other, and are not defined psychologically but circumstantially: *The Flies* (1943), *No Exit* (1944), *Dirty Hands* (1948), among others.

1945 – today

154

and elsewhere, the terrrible power of the bombs that destroyed Hiroshima and Nagasaki, and, for many, the failure of the communist utopia under the Stalinist terror destroyed hope for the "dawn of humanity" in the middle of the century.

The existential philosophers and dramatists Jean-Paul Sartre and Albert Camus described the world at this point as a metaphysical no man's land in which mankind is condemned to the freedom of having to give meaning to his own existence. The only hope, for the existentialists, of giving meaning to life lay in a perpetual struggle against absurdity.

The search for the meaning of life—an endeavor bound always to remain futile, but that must never be given up—unifies into a "movement" such stylistically different works as those by dramatists such as Arthur Adamov, Harold Pinter, Jean Genet, Eugène Ionesco, Edward Albee, and Samuel Beckett. Their "theater of the absurd" paradigmatically presented the loneliness of mankind in a world devoid of extrinsic meaning; these authors renounced realistic psychological character depictions and traditional plot development. They turned instead to parody and the grotesque, offended provocatively against the "laws" of reality, and borrowed strongly from the surrealists' aesthetic. The sense of being lost and the existential angst of mankind are revealed most clearly in the dialogue. These are characters who do not communicate, but rather spin inwardly with tirades of half-truths and clichés. What Ionesco characterized as their "auto-

Irish-born playwright **Samuel Beckett** (1906–89) lived and worked from 1937 until his death in Paris. In 1969 he received the Nobel Prize for Literature. In addition to *Waiting for Godot*, he wrote *Endgame* (1957), *Krapp's Last Tape* (1958), and *Happy Days* (1961), among many others.

No one in the theater has been more critical of the American way of life than **Edward Albee** (1928–). Albee started his career with a series of absurd one-act plays, but his greatest success remains the scathingly realistic *Who's Afraid of Virginia Woolf?* (1962).

British playwright **Harold Pinter** (1930–) worked as actor, author, and director. In plays such as *The Caretaker* (1960), *The Homecoming* (1965), and *The Birthday Party* he plumbs the absurdity of daily existence and the strangeness that lurks in the ordinary.

Eugène Ionesco's *The Chairs* in a 1956 Paris Studio production.

1945 – today

The Romanian **Eugène Ionesco** (1912–94) lived in France after 1938 and wrote his major works in French, since 1970 as a member of the Académie Française. He earned international success with absurdist dramas such as *The Bald Soprano* (1950) and *Rhinoceros* (1959).

Dario Fo (1926–), cheerfully anarchic actor and writer of farces, represents the quintessence of European political folk theater. His clear political position stirs up controversy and garners both legal indictments and performance prohibitions. He performs in Italian with a changing ensemble.

Giorgio Strehler (1921–) founded the first successful "teatro stabile" in Italy in 1947. The Piccolo Teatro in Milan, which receives slightly more than $4 million annually, is the most heavily subsidized theater in Italy. By comparison, Cologne, Germany, received a subsidy of almost $5.4 million in 1994.

matized speech," leading nowhere, expresses their total alienation from their surroundings, their fellow human beings, and their selves.

The economics of theater

Today, for the price of a television set (and many homes in the United States have more than one), and perhaps a cable television service, entertainment and "culture" can be delivered into the living room easily and cheaply. Theater, on the other hand, is not only labor-intensive but must be re-created anew every day. It has become an extremely expensive undertaking. Noncommercial theater has always depended on the support of wealthy patrons. But today, set against the immense entertainment industry worldwide (to which many theaters also belong), theater is dependent for its very existence on public subsidy, of one form or another.

Specific cultural, social, and political developments have led to completely different forms of organization and management in Europe and in countries where Europe's cultural influence has been felt. Italy is, as ever, the land of itinerant troupes. Alongside a good dozen state and community theaters with resident companies stand an immense number of barely subsidized groups that play throughout the country.

The theater life of England and France is still largely concentrated in the urban centers of London and Paris. London's West End is famous for its more than 40 commercial private theaters offering a broad spectrum of productions from cheap revues and Christmas pantomimes to the classical repertoire to

The Royal Shakespeare Company plays in two London theaters built specially for them. With around $1.4 million, the RSC is the second most subsidized theater in England, next to the National Theater. This is a production photo from Peter Brook's 1978 *King Lear*.

ambitious new works by contemporary authors to Broadway imports. State funding offers support for only a few large companies like the Royal Shakespeare Company (with two homes, one in Stratford-upon-Avon, and the relatively new Barbizon Center) and the National Theatre (in its modern complex on the South Bank of the Thames). A centralized Arts Council supports around 60 permanent repertory theaters in the provinces.

France has been trying since 1945 to decentralize the theater by establishing state-subsidized Centres Dramatiques in the provinces. The lion's share of the funds, however, still flows into the five large national theaters, four of which are located in Paris.

Lord Laurence Olivier (1907–1989) is considered by many *the* leading British actor of the 20th century; he was the head of the National Theater from 1963 to 1973. Olivier is shown here as John Rice, the sleazy comic in John Osborne's 1957 play, *The Entertainer*.

In today's Germany, the public is supplied with theater across the board. In the 1994–95 season, the German Bühnenverein (Stage Association) numbered 788 stages throughout

The theater collective Théâtre du Soleil, founded in 1964 by Ariane Mnouchkine, became the most successful French theater in spite of extremely modest governmental support. The troupe's home is in the halls of the Cartoucherie, an old Paris weapons factory. This photo is from a 1991 production of Aeschylus's *Agamemnon*.

In 1945 many of Germany's theaters lay in dust and ashes. The construction and reconstruction of numerous state playhouses reflects the country's difficult struggle for cultural identity after the war.

the country, of which 404 are almost fully subsidized at the city, state, or national level. A number of the private theaters (141) are operated noncommercially in the public interest, and also receive public funding. In contrast, therefore, to the 243 commercially operated theaters, the majority of German stages are free from commercial pressures and can devote themselves to more artistic pursuits.

"There's no business like show business"

While the German public is willing to invest over three billion marks a year (more than $2 billion) in tax revenue in their public theaters—that is, more than $100 per visitor—the Americans have managed like no other culture in the world to turn theater into a business. What Hollywood is to films, Broadway is to the theater. Along the legendary "White Way" in the heart of New York City, stars and managers set the tone, and the financial stakes are quite high. Approximately thirty theaters with an average of 1,000 seats

The Berliner Schaubühne has operated since 1970 as a collective in which all members have an equal voice in policy decisions; this democratic structure leaves a particular mark on the productions. Under the artistic direction (1970–92) of Peter Stein, the Schaubühne has become the leading theater in Germany, and it is one of the most heavily subsidized private theaters. This production photo is from *Kalldewey*, a farce by Botho Strauss, directed by Luc Bondy.

1945 – today

each compete intensely for the more or less well-to-do middle-class public.

The first theaters opened on Broadway in the 19th century, preying both formally and thematically on European theater. But from the beginning, the "long run" system where a series of productions follow each other, sometimes for years on end (basically until the audience has tired of the show and the producers decide they can make more money with some other production), and the cultivation of the star system have distinguished the American system from its European-style beginnings. In the early years, great mimes and singers from Europe—Eleonora Duse, Sarah Bernhardt, Edmund Kean—were brought over as sensational attractions and box offices were swamped by the demand. At the same time, the newer country, with its newer traditions, struggled to discover and establish its own theatrical voice.

The golden years of Broadway intersect with those of American drama. Between 1930 and 1960, daring producers succeeded in bringing challenging drama to the stage along with the usual fluff—variety shows, the spectacular Ziegfeld Follies, the remnants of vaudeville traditions, the dramatically thin, but musically rich musicals of Irving Berlin, George Gershwin, and Cole Porter (among many, many others).

As with every other aspect of American culture, the American theater sought to create its own traditions. The earliest successes in serious dramatic literature came in the ostensibly social and psychological realism of writers like Eugene O'Neill,

In 1993 the Berlin Senate decided to close the Schiller Theater due to the demands of general budget reductions. The decision unleashed nationwide discussion of the explosion of costs and the death of the theater in Germany.

The extremely popular Volkstheater Millowitsch was founded in Cologne in 1896; since then it has been passed down from father to son. It has prospered without state subsidies but, in spite of constantly sold-out houses, relies for income on television and other commercial advertisements before performances.

1945 – today

The Palace Theater on Broadway.

Tennessee Williams (1911–83) chronicled the feelings and outlooks of life in the face of the Great Depression, economic troubles, and unemployment. *The Glass Menagerie* (1945), *A Streetcar Named Desire* (1947), and *Cat on a Hot Tin Roof* (1955), with their portrayals of unstable characters who tend toward destruction and self-destruction in an unsympathetic world, are considered American classics, often produced and widely studied.

Arthur Miller (1915–), the moralist of the American theater, questions how the individual pursuit of happiness can be reconciled with social responsibility. In the psychologically realistic drama, *Death of a Salesman* (1948), he shows the tragedy of a little man who cannot admit to his failure to attain the American dream.

Clifford Odets, and Lillian Hellman. O'Neill, the son of a successful Shakespearean actor, James O'Neill, established himself as the first "genuine" American playwright—first to achieve worldwide recognition and success with dramas written in a distinctly American idiom. Probably his most famous work, *Long Day's Journey into Night* (1939–41) is a milestone in world theater, an intensely personal, relentlessly self-reflective drama about a family's struggles with their demons, illusions, and addictions (very definitely based on the playwright's own life). Always experimenting, from his realist beginnings to his more symbolic and Expressionist works (for example, *The Emperor Jones*), O'Neill attempted a range of styles, and was unfettered by commercial constraints or conventions—his plays were often far longer than most audiences (or critics) were accustomed to sitting, but it was clear that O'Neill was writing from an expressive inner need, and this, perhaps more than anything else, marks him as an American dramatist. It is difficult to imagine the subsequent history of American drama without his influence.

Broadway had proven a home for O'Neill and his successors. Thornton Wilder with *Our Town* and *The Skin of Our Teeth*, Arthur Miller with *Death of a Salesman, The Crucible*, and *A View from the Bridge*, and Tennessee Williams with *The Glass Menagerie, A Streetcar Named Desire*, and many other plays all met with success here, all contributing to a growing theater tradition. All, also, were sought by Hollywood, which continues to call on their works for film and television

1945 – today

productions. In the beginning of the 1960s, the Broadway production of *Who's Afraid of Virginia Woolf?* added the name of Edward Albee to this august company.

Today's Broadway theater posters mostly announce entertainment—Neil Simon comedies and Andrew Lloyd Webber musicals. The cost of mounting a musical production on Braodway today runs into several million dollars, and every year, it seems, new productions are quoted as costing some new record amount, in an effort to

compete with the hype that surrounds other shows. The controlling force of commercial theater on Broadway is the producer; every production needs financial backers who invest in the production for a percentage of profits. To draw investors, producers must assemble an attractive package of composers, choreographers, and stars. The production company then actually rents an available theater—hence, "theater owner" in the United States ought not to be confused with creative endeavor. When the financing is secured, hundreds of actors and actresses go through the process of auditions, not called "cattle calls" for nothing. American produc-

tions are famous for their dancing, music, and acting. Actual rehearsal time is usually only three to six weeks—a grueling schedule. Through a series of previews and tryouts, the performance is tested on the public. Often the

Fred Astaire and Claire Luce in *The Gay Divorcée* (1932).

Marlon Brando with Jessica Tandy in Tennessee Williams' *A Streetcar Named Desire* (1947). Brando's unforgettable portrayal of Stanley Kowalski, re-created in the 1952 film of the play, brought him, and his Actors Studio method acting, to the attention of Hollywood.

Julie Andrews in *Camelot* (1960).

Liza Minnelli in *The Rink* (1984).

1945 – today

161

Gene Hackman, Richard Dreyfus, and Glenn Close, all popular movie stars, returned to Broadway in the 1992 play, *Death and the Maiden*, by Ariel Dorfmann.

total production is reworked, because when the play opens on Broadway, the reviews of theater critics can very well determine its success.

Everybody everywhere knows about Broadway. But Broadway is not the be-all and end-all of American theater. Not even in New York City. There is also "Off-Broadway," where productions are mounted on a somewhat smaller scale, where theatrical experiments test the waters of the New York audience, where the stakes are not quite so high. Many a Broadway production has started Off-Broadway, and while it may remain the ultimate goal for an Off-Broadway producer to have his or her production make the move uptown, Off-Broadway still seems to offer a little more freedom for the exploration of theatrical possibilities.

New York also boasts the "Off-Off-Broadway" of semiprofessionals and amateurs, offering works that would have no chance from a commercial point of view: experimental and political pieces. The artistic freedom of Off-Off-Broadway, coinciding with trends in the arts toward the conceptual, gave rise to the "happening," a multimedia show in which the boundaries between actors and audience, like those between music, graphic arts, and theater, are dissolved.

In spite of steadily rising ticket prices—the average top seat cost $65 in 1995—Broadway theaters that present modern drama rarely make a profit. The union wages are too high, rent and advertising too expensive. Even "successes" like Tony Kushner's *Angels in America*, which opened on Broadway in 1993, and won the Tony Award for its two parts in two consecutive years, as well as the Pulitzer Prize, can fail on Broadway. The play was closed in December 1994 with a loss of

Broadway's favored son has always been the musical. Poster for *Cats* by Andrew Lloyd Webber (and T.S. Eliot), which opened in New York (after smashing success in London) in 1981.

$660,000, in spite of full houses and the Pulitzer prize. The producers assembled a touring company, however, which brought the two-part drama to regional commercial theaters throughout the country. This is a route often chosen by producers, to try to recoup some of their investment, to keep worthy productions in front of the public eye, and to make more money. Many of the larger Broadway productions (*Cats, Phantom of the Opera, Les Miserables,* or the old standard shows, *Guys and Dolls* or *The Sound of Music*) will send touring companies around the country, and/or the world, while the Broadway production is still running.

It is generally to Off-Broadway and to regional theater—in Boston, Baltimore, Chicago, Minneapolis, Los Angeles—that one must look for new, artistically ambitious drama. Funded by private grants and donations as well as the National Endowment for the Arts and state and local arts councils, affiliated with universities and drama schools, forming part of art centers in haphazard spaces to more elaborate complexes, mounting seasons of repertory programs that include new works, classical works, experimental works, international works—these theaters struggle in a climate of austerity and often political resistance to continue to forge a vital tradition of theater in America.

What should the theater do?

There is no question that the expanding dominance of the mass media has put pressure on the traditional theater, in both theory and practice. First, the advent of film overshadowed any claims the theater might make to perfect illusionism; later, movies and television overtook the theater as the most popular, and more lucrative, form of public entertainment. Even education has turned to first film and now video for instructional aids, and poli-

Most great Broadway hits are eventually made into great, and not so great, movies.

The name of the Bread and Puppet Theater of New York (founded in 1961) speaks its philosophy: the integration of life and art. Playing in open rooms or out of doors, the larger-than-life puppets usually do without speech and borrow mythical symbols from various cultures.

1945 – today

The San Francisco Mime Troupe (founded in 1959) unites political agitation with theatrical entertainment. Run as a collective, it draws on the commedia dell'arte tradition, and tours extensively, often in outdoor venues, such as parks.

"CLOWNPOWER is love and love is only another label for hope." In the 1970s Jango Edwards became the leading figure in the CLOWNPOWER movement, which is something of a cross between circus show and political cabaret.

1945 – today

tics has turned to those same media for propaganda. These industries—which may or may not deserve to be labeled "arts"—have drained the theater of the creative talents that, in a previous age, might have turned to it for expression. Those who would enlighten or revolutionize or otherwise affect the world have turned to other media, other venues, other methods.

The theater of the late 20th century seems to be caught in an ongoing crisis. Government funding is limited, and is not allocated with no strings attached, while only commercially oriented theater seems to have bounced back from the enormous drop in theatergoing that followed the widespread popularity of television.

The entrepreneurs who once offered pomp and spectacle at the theaters of Europe in bygone days because that was what the audience wanted are not themselves a bygone phenomenon. The American principles of show business practice—mounting large and expensive musical productions like *Cats, Starlight Express, The Phantom of the Opera* (all of which originated in London's West End, but turned their sights across the Atlantic where the real profits lie), in specially designed theaters, are making their way to Europe. No different from audiences through the millenia, today's leisure society demands mere "entertainment," and in the face of such demand, the theater of entertainment has been able to hold its own. Those moments when art and entertainment seem to coincide in the same works are unpredictable, but there is no reason to suppose that they won't continue as well. With the firm entrenchment of film and the electronic media, live theater most likely will be perpetuated for a very good reason—because people who love it will continue to engage in it. And out of such commitment, art will emerge.

International independent theater

The 1960s marked a cultural, political, and social turning point. While the Beatles stormed America, and the United States saw its most widespread disaffection to date in protests against the Vietnam War, young people working in the theater everywhere looked for a new meaning in the old medium of the theater beyond simple pleasure or cultural mediocrity. They rejected traditional aesthetic forms as well as the work practices and business principles of the established commercial and cultural theater.

This renewal focused on a return to theater's origins. Those who rejected the mainstream defined the performance of a play as an independent medium of interpersonal communication. The "independent theater" of the 1960s experimented with audience and actor exchanging roles; it actively involved the public in the plot, proclaimed the play as a medium for the players' self-knowledge, and strove to lift the barriers between life and art. In the search for new space and speech for the theater, independent theater looked to surviving forms of various ethnic cult theaters, to non-European traditions, to the vital commedia dell'arte, and to the political theater of the 1920s.

It is impossible to define a simple stylistic direction for the independent theaters. The political agitation of the San Francisco Mime Troupe is as significant as the mythically symbolic Bread and Puppet Theater, the happy anarchism of Clown Jango Edwards, and the ritualized gesture language of Julian Beck's Living Theater.

"Poor" theater

It was in the 1960s that the heretofore obscure theories of Antonin Artaud (and his notions of a

Antonin Artaud (1896–1948) was an actor, director, and theater manager, but is known mostly as an early theorist of the modern theater. At his Théâtre de la cruaté he produced only one play, *Les Cenci*, in which he himself appeared.

Artaud's influence reached to Japan where, in the 1950s, the young author and director Shuji Terayama established one of the first experimental theater groups that renounced tradition and convention in both theater and society, and sought to develop new conceptions of theatrical space.

Jerzy Grotowski (1933–) studied acting and direction in Cracow and Moscow, and became the most important experimental theatrical artist in Poland. Grotowski has written his own scenes based on literary models, including *Dr. Faustus* (from Marlowe) and *Study on Hamlet* (from Shakespeare).

The Odin Teatret, the internationally acclaimed Danish experimental theater, was established in 1964 by Jerzy Grotowski's pupil Eugenio Barba. The Odin has developed into a laboratory of the performing arts where drama, pedagogy, and scholarship are closely bound together.

"The act of the player ... is an invitation to the spectator. This act may be compared to the most deeply felt exchange between two people in the act of love." This photo is from Grotowski's production of Calderón de la Barca's *The Resolute Prince*.

1945 – today

theater of cruelty) took hold in the theater world. The most serious realization and development of Artaud's insistence on a nonrational, nonliterary, unbounded aesthetic experience are in the work of the Polish director Jerzy Grotowski, who left Poland in 1982 for the United States. From the beginning, Grotowski showed little interest in the art of staging as a synthesis of different artistic genres. Rather, he was convinced that everything that one might portray on the stage could be said with the language of the human body.

Instead of a wealthy theater that goes to great lengths to imitate movies and television, Grotowski wanted a "poor" theater—without props, costumes, decoration, or stage machinery. In the center of his work stands the actor (or actress), who would need intense physical and psychological training. From his players, Grotowski demands seriousness, honor, submission, and self-revelation. The rehearsal of literary roles serves his ensemble only as a vehicle for coming to terms with their own identity. Ultimately, for this ritual self-discovery, the presence of an audience is superfluous.

Living theater means life

"They perform because the act and fact of performing corresponds to a great shared need. They are in search of meaning in their lives, and in a sense even if there were no audiences, they would still have to perform, because the theatrical event is the climax and centre of their search." So Peter Brook (in *The Empty Space*) describes the "Off-Off" ensemble, the Living Theater. For the founders of the Living Theater, Judith Malina and Julian Beck, who died in 1985, artistic and private existence were inseparable. They lived and

The Living Theatre, *Paradise Now* (1968).

The Living Theatre, with Julian Beck at the top, in a scene from *Antigone* (1982).

worked collectively with their troupe, developed their plays and productions as a team, and became the model for a whole generation of free theater ensembles. Their theater and their lives flowed together in a single show of opposition to middle-class small-mindedness and repression. They adopted slogans like, "The only artistic creation that interests me is my life" and "We can't change anything except ourselves."

The Living Theater's artistic and political statements were so radical that the troupe often came up against the law. Pacifists by conviction, they refused to pay taxes to a government at war and spent time in prison for their beliefs. In 1968, the authorities in Avignon intervened during a performance of *Paradise Now* when the Living Theater called upon the audience to reject all forms of state authority, to throw off their clothes, and by so doing show that it was possible to make a society free from oppression.

Living Theater is the "poor theater" of naked players; it is ritualized body language and at the

After a 1977 performance of *Seven Meditations against Political Masochism*, Julian Beck was arrested in Munich and accused of slandering the state for the play's inclusion of Germany among the countries depicted as engaging in political torture.

1945 – today

same time highly political. Among their most impressive works from the 1960s is *The Brig*, a drastic portrayal of a day in an American military prison. It is a vehement rejection of the military power structure and of the vicious circle of physical and psychological violence.

Theater as food

While the experiments of the 1960s aimed at breaking down the barriers between art and life, between audience and actors, the 1970s reclaimed the notion that watching a play could be a rational and active form of understanding. English director Peter Brook imbued the theories of Artaud and Grotowski with a traditional understanding of theater as presentation: theater that no longer distinguishes itself from life, felt Brook, has no meaning.

In 1962, Peter Brook mounted Shakespeare's *King Lear* for the Royal Shakespeare Company, with Diana Rigg as Cordelia and Paul Scofield as Lear.

The special quality of the theater for Brook lies in its ability to present life in concentrated form. Because the majority of life escapes human sense, the stage is the ideal place to make the invisible visible and to make it easier to decode life. Brook considers the theater the last place where human dreams can still be conveyed, and speaks therefore of the theater as a kind of food that is as necessary for mankind as eating and procreation.

For the stage to work against the general atrophy of the power to imagine, theatrical language must constantly grow. Theater must surprise the

In 1975 Peter Brook's international troupe took *The Ik*, about the extermination of the native Americans, on a world tour.

public and therefore avoid unquestioned aesthetic convention and routine (what Brook would call the "Deadly Theatre"). In 1971 Brook, with his newly founded International Centre of Theatre Research, produced *Orghast*, written by the English poet Ted Hughes, in an ancient Persian ceremonial language, consisting totally of sounds.

Peter Brook (1925–) published his lectures on the theater in *The Empty Space*, which has become a bible for young theatrical artists.

Brook staged many a successful production during his tenure at the Royal Shakespeare Company, where he served for a time as co-artistic director. His productions of *King Lear*, of the

groundbreaking *Marat/ Sade* by Peter Weiss, of *A Midsummer Night's Dream* à la commedia dell'arte, among many others, toured throughout the world, including in non-English-speaking, non-Western countries, and set a new standard for production.

The nine-hour *Mahābhārata* was first presented between sunset and sunrise in a quarry near Avignon, France, in 1985.

His next experiment led Brook to undertake a theater safari through Africa with his independent group, where he confronted the actors with a public that had no ideal of European theater to test the effectiveness of his new theater language. In the middle of the 1970s Brook and his international ensemble settled down in the Parisian Théâtre Bouffles du Nord. His productions took place in "an empty space" without scenery or other visual effects in order to concentrate attention firmly on the acting.

A scene from the *Mahābhārata*.

The opportunity of the theater

In the midst of all the ideological and aesthetic variety of the international independent

"They say that my pieces are gruesome. I am only showing life as it is." Since 1978, the Compagnie Jérôme Deschamps of Paris, named after its founder and director, has developed its own unique grotesque style for the portrayal of everyday events.

theater, there is one common point. The proponents of the theater redefined theater art as a free field for experiences which, in an age when work life holds few human values and communication is ever more alienating as it is increasingly consigned to electronic media, are otherwise unavailable to the average person. By placing the means of presentation squarely on the shoulders of the performer, and her or his ability to function as a creative agent, the interaction between performers and public again took center stage and the spectator was transformed into an active co-creator of the work. This allowed theater to make good use of the particular freedom that it has to offer an audience. The audience has no effect on screen (large or small) performances, but the theater gives the audience the freedom to choose the direction of its own gaze and to exercise its own imagination.

Canadian director Robert Lepage sees the future of the theater in its obvious unreality, its essential fictiveness: "Theater is concerned with lies. ... Film and television are seen as the media of truth. Nonetheless they lie constantly, ... suggest closeness and participation ... as if they were the third eye in the head of the viewer. ... As Picasso said, art lies, in order to speak the truth more clearly."

The Catalanian group Els Joglars (founded in 1964) is the oldest independent ensemble in Spain. Under Franco, the troupe displayed courageous political opposition in the face of censorship, prohibition, and imprisonment.

The most recent theatrical wonder of the 1990s is London's celebrated Théâtre de Complicité, acclaimed by reviewers throughout Europe. The Théâtre de Complicité exemplifies the qualities of the independent theater. The troupe's director, Simon McBurney, has gathered an international company of the best-trained actors who dominate the stage with creative fantasy and physical expression. The critic Renate Klett enthusiasically praised their productions in *Theater heute*: "They are spectacular and quick and wonderfully musical; they thrive on contact with the public, from the amazing directness and corporality of the actors and actresses; they create pictures and dramas and worlds out of nothing—only fantasy counts, and the willingness to trust it."

McBurney is molding a new kind of theater experience out of classics like Shakespeare's *The Winter's Tale* or Friedrich Dürrenmatt's *The Visit of the Old Lady*. He uses improvisation with his company to rework texts and create new pieces. His passionate commitment to the theater underscores the particular value and opportunity of the medium in the next millenia:

"Theater always takes place in the present, not the future, like film, where all that is important is what will happen next. Theater happens now, in this moment, and then it is past and can't be held back—except in memory. That is what is old-fashioned and wonderful about the theater, that it insists on the present. ... Our society recognizes only the past and the future—my investment from yesterday will bring me profit tomorrow—and that is why a society that knows only one goal, namely money and gain, wants to have nothing to do with the theater. But this extreme materialism has created a social desert, and our need to experience something together is more pressing than ever. Theater is water and bread."

Simon McBurney (1957-) was a student of Jacques Lecoq in Paris and acted with Jérôme Deschamps. In 1983 he founded the touring company Théâtre de Complicité in London.

In 1995 the Théâtre de Complicité produced *Out of a House Walked a Man* from a text by Daniil Charms at London's National Theater.

1945 – today

Glossary

Act: a major division of a play, structured in space or time; a spatial division necessitates a change of setting (with a raising of the curtain after the scene is set). In content, the act corresponds to a further level of development of the plot. As a rule, an act consists of several scenes or entrances. The five-act division occurred first in Seneca and was adopted as a norm by neoclassical theater (and retroactively imposed, for example, on Shakespeare's plays). According to Gustav Freytag's *Technique of Drama* (1863), a five-act drama is structured as follows: introductory exposition (I), increasing of complexity (II), climax (III), decisive turning point (IV), catastrophe or solution (V). The 19th century brought the development of a three- or four-act structure; modern playwrights have developed the one-act play and increasingly ignore the division into acts in favor of other dramatic forms.

Agon: a contest for tragic poets in ancient Greek theater.

Alternation: alternately filling one role with two actors.

Apron: the front of the stage toward the audience; originally at a slant allowing access to the stage from the house.

Bourgeois tragedy: tragic genre of the 18th and 19th centuries in which the action is set for the first time in a bourgeois, or middle class, milieu. This development mirrors the rise of the middle class and its increasing political voice.

Catharsis: (Greek = cleansing). Central term in Aristotle's theory of tragedy. In the various interpretations of the *Poetics*, catharsis was often misunderstood as a moral purification of the audience *through* fear and pity. The consensus today is that Aristotle meant a purification *from* pity and fear, that is, tragedy as a release function in the sense of providing a liberation from the troubling conditions.

Cathurn: originally the flat shoe used in Greek tragedy; acquired a raised sole in the Hellenistic period, and developed to an eight-inch platform shoe in the Roman theater.

Character roles: in the commedia dell'arte, it was normal for a character to specialize in one role for life, for example, that of Pantalone. From these permanent figures, character types like the hero, the lover, the intriguer, the bon vivant, and so on developed in the 18th and 19th centuries. Actors played these various roles according to their age and outward appearance, and normally in an ensemble specialized in one comic and one tragic character role. The wages of the actor were determined according to the types. The development of modern drama with its complexity of character has made the character roles almost superfluous, though the term is still employed in Hollywood where a man may be labeled a "character actor" if he does not fit the ruling standard for a leading man (and the same, of course, for an actress).

Charge: a normally comic supporting role, requiring exaggerated characterization.

Deus ex machina: (Latin = god out of a machine). In various Greek tragedies, a hopeless conflict is resolved through the intervention of a god who arrives on some sort of stage machine normally lowered from aloft.

Director's theater: modern theatrical approach whereby the production becomes the artistic creation of the director who shapes the text, the acting, the setting, and the music into a unified whole.

Distancing: a theatrical means found in all cultures to present the familiar in a new, often comic, light. In Brecht's theory, distancing or alienation becomes centrally important: all theatrical effects,

Glossary

from the construction of the drama to the lighting of the play to the artistry of the actors aim at distancing what is being portrayed in order to motivate the audience to an active, independent, and critical perspective on the events.

Dramatics: along with the *lyric* and the *epic*, according to Goethe, one of the three basic forms of poetry; also a general literary term for all forms of play texts in dialogue: tragedy, comedy, tragicomedy, melodrama, farce, etc.

Dramaturge: artistic and scholarly colleague of the director and the manager of the theater, responsible for various duties relating to the program, including coordination with authors, publicity, and, with the director, the development of the directorial concept.

Dramaturgy: external form and internal structure of a drama.

Epilogue: speech directed to the audience at the end of a play.

Estates: ancient tragedy and French neoclassical tragedy treated the fates of only the upper classes, while the lower classes tumbled about in comedy.

Extemporaries: improvised variations from the written text to cover gaps in the text, to draw the audience spontaneously into the play, or to demonstrate the virtuosity of the actors; during periods of theater

censorship, extemps provided room for references to recent events or political commentary.

Extras: also called *supernumeraries*, players in nonspeaking or very small roles.

Fidelity to text: conservative demand for performances that attempt to follow the supposed intentions of the author or of the period in which he wrote, thereby denying that every presentation of a stage text is an interpretation influenced by the time of the performance.

Fire curtain: iron sheet that can be lowered in case of fire between the stage and the theater; introduced after a fire in the Viennese Ring Theater in 1881 in which 450 people died.

Flats: wooden frames covered with stretched canvas or paper to represent scenery on the proscenium stage; the frames were paired on opposite sides of the stage, and together with the painted backdrop, created a perspectival stage with three-dimensional depth.

Flies: the space over the stage where parts of the scenery (flats, backdrops, etc.) hang on ropes, to be lowered onto the stage as necessary.

Foyer: waiting hall, or lobby, for the public before and after the performance and during intermissions; introduced in the 18th century when the theater became

a forum for the middle class.

Gestic: language of gesture and body movement

Hose roles: man's part for a female actress; female characters appearing in boys' or men's clothing to increase the comic situation or sexual tension; The confusions and double entendres occasioned by the role changes were especially popular during the Renaissance and baroque period, when women first appeared on stage.

Illusion, theater of: refined, technical stage effects, natural stage setting, and acting techniques to make the audience ignore the "fourth wall" and forget that it is watching a play. The illusionist style peaked with the naturalistic theater.

Impromptu play: stage performance without written dialogue, based only on briefly noted plot developments; the performers improvise the play.

Premiere: the first performance of a play or of a new production of a play.

Principal: leader of an itinerant troupe, usually an entrepreneur, business manager, and actor.

Production, staging: setting up and rehearsals of a play, also the end-product of the work; the complete presentation as shaped by the director.

Prologue: introductory words to a performance spoken by the author or an actor.

Glossary ... A brief overview of theater history

Prompter: text reader who follows the text and stands ready to remind actors of lines in case of memory gaps. Many stages are equipped with a prompting box, a low floor in the middle of the apron, where the prompter remains hidden from the public.

Props: smaller, movable parts of the scenery or objects used by the performer.

Revolving stage: circular area in the floor of the stage, or a built-up level, that can be rotated for set changes or dramatic effect.

Simultaneous staging: In contrast to the single or the successive stage, the various settings of the play are built next to each other on the stage.

Stilbühne ("art stage"): aesthetic countermovement at the turn of the century to the naturalistic theater of trompe l'oeil and realistic props; normally an almost empty, single-setting stage controlled by the actors and a few stylized props indicating the time of the action.

Strikings: textual omissions in a production either for reasons of staging (secondary characters, longer texts) or for conceptual purposes.

Sunken stage: a part of the floor of the stage can be raised or lowered by equipment hidden under the stage; favorite historical effect for the appearance of ghosts and devils.

Theater pedagogy: general term for various measures to introduce theater visitors (especially children and young adults) to the theater; includes activities before and after the performance for the laity. Originally, however, the term referred to any of the various professional training programs for the theater.

Theatron: place for the audience in the ancient Greek theater.

Thrust stage: a stage whose apron extends beyond the proscenium arch into the audience, who may, in effect, be seated on three sides of the action.

Unities: The classical unities of action, place, and time. The French neoclassicists raised these to a poetic norm, based on a misreading of Aristotle's Poetics. Aristotle demanded only the unity of plot, which is the carrying through of a basic motive without episode and side plots, and observed that the performance time of most of the plots corresponded to the real timing of the events, but he did not derive from this a "law" regarding the unity of time. Aristotle does not speak of unity of place; the later insistence on it severely hampered the dramatic development of the poets and became one of the central issues of dramaturgy.

2000–1500 B.C. Mystery plays in ancient Egypt

534 B.C. Thespis is probably the first victor in the tragedy contest of the Great Dionysia

486 B.C. First comic productions in Athens

472 B.C. Aeschylus introduces a second actor in his play The Persians

442–41 B.C. Sophocles introduces a third actor in Antigone

425 B.C. The first comic victory of Aristophanes; golden age of Attic Old Comedy

335 B.C. Aristotle writes his Poetics

240 B.C. Introduction of theater presentations in the Roman city festivals, the ludi romani, in which Livius Andronicus brings a Greek drama on the stage for the first time

204 B.C. Premiere of Plautus's Miles Gloriosus

160 B.C. Premiere of Terence's Adelphoe

4 B.C.–65 A.D. Seneca

529 A.D. Roman Emperor Justinian orders the closing of all theaters

750 Chinese Emperor Xuangzong establishes the world's first theater school in his Pear Garden

930 Introduction in France of the Quem Quaeritis

A brief overview of theater history

skit, forerunner of the Easter liturgy performances

ca. 935–1000 Abbess Hrotsvitha composes six comedies to counterbalance the immoral comedies of Terence

ca. 1000 Spread of the shadow play throughout Asia

12th c. Theatrical additions to the Easter celebration develop into an Easter play that is increasingly performed outside the church

ca. 1180 First production of the religious *Spectacula* in London

1205 Performance of Jehan Bodel's *St. Nickolas Play* in Arras indicates the secularization of spiritual dramas through liberation from the liturgy and unusual theatrical form

mid-14th c. Creation of the Japanese Nō plays

1414 Rediscovery of Vitruvius's architectural studies of Roman theater buildings

1448 Earliest evidence of the presentation of *Sacre Rappresentazioni* in Florence

1471–75 First division of Latin dramas into scenes in Rome

1486 First performance of Plautus's *Menaechmi* in Italian at the court of Ferrara

1494–1576 Meistersinger Hans Sachs composes more than 200 secular dramatic works—

carnival pieces, tragedies, and comedies

1508 Premiere of *La Cassaria* by Ariosto is one of the first theater presentations with a perspectival set

1516–19 Gil Vincente, founder of the Portuguese theater, composes three *Autos das Barcas do Inferno, do Purgatório, da Gloria*

1520 Premiere of Machiavelli's *La Mandragola* in Florence

1523 Beginning of the humanistic school theater in Germany

1545 Notarized contract in Padua is the oldest witness for the establishment of a troupe of professional actors

1547 Well-documented *Passion from Valencienes* stands as one of the last great theater events of the Middle Ages

1568 Massimo Troiano composes the earliest surviving written scenario of a commedia dell' arte for performance at a Bavarian court

1570– Corral theaters are constructed throughout Spain

1573 Isabella Andreini, the most famous of the first actresses of modern history, stars in the male leading role of Tasso's *Aminta*

1576 James Burbage opens the first public theater in London

1587 Christopher Marlowe's *Tamburlaine*

the Great introduces "Marlowe's mighty line," that is, blank (iambic pentameter, nonrhyming) verse

1584 Opening of the Teatro Olimpico in Vicenza with a production of Sophocles' *Oedipus the King*

1592 First recorded notice of the London actor William Shakespeare

1599 With the completion of *Julius Caesar*, Shakespeare begins his series of great tragedies: *Hamlet* (1601); *Othello* (1604); *King Lear* and *Macbeth* (1606)

1605 Ben Jonson, *Volpone*

1618 Lope de Vega writes *Fuente Ovejuna* (The burning village)

1623 Printing of the First Folio of Shakespeare's plays

1628 Opening in Parma of the Teatre Farnese, which uses movable flats for the first time

1629 Prohibition against the appearance of women in Japanese Kabuki theater; after 1652 the prohibition also applies to boys

1630 Tirso de Molina, *The Trickster from Seville*, first dramatization of the Don Juan legend

1635 Calderón de la Barca completes *Life Is a Dream* and becomes head of the court theater Buen Retiro and court dramatist

1637 Overwhelming public success for Corneille's *Le Cid*

A brief overview of theater history

1642 Puritans close the theaters in England

1653 Louis XIV appears in the royal *Ballet de la nuit* as the Sun King

1660 With the restoration of the monarchy, and the reopening of the theaters, women appear for the first time on English stages

1664 Molière's troupe premieres the first comedy of Racine, *La Thébaïde ou les Frères ennemis*; Molière's *Tartuffe* is banned by the censor

1666–67 The opera *Il Pomo d'oro* by Antonio Cesti, presented in Vienna on the occasion of the marriage of Leopold I and Margarita, becomes one of the most spectacular productions of the baroque theater, thanks to the settings of Burnacini

1675 William Wycherley, *The Country Wife*

1677 Racine, *Phaedre*

1680 Founding of the Comédie Française

1699 First performance license for a theater on New York's Broadway

1700 William Congreve, *The Way of the World*

1703 Chikamatsu Monzaemon, one of the most popular dramatists in Japan, composes *Sonezaki shinju* (Double suicide in Sonezaki), the first social drama of the Japanese theater

1731 In the melodrama *The London Merchant* by Lillo, a middle-class citizen first appears as the victim of a tragic fate

1737 Mrs. Neuber bans Hans Wurst from the German stage

1746 Carlo Goldoni, *Servant of Two Masters*

1769 Failure of the Hamburg theater enterprise: the first German National Theater goes bankrupt: in Vienna the defenders of "regular theater" succeed in banning impromptu drama

1775 Richard Brinsley Sheridan's comedy, *The Rivals*, introduces the memorable Mrs. Malaprop

1779 Gotthold Ephraim Lessing, *Nathan the Wise*

1782 Friedrich Schiller's *The Robbers* is a great success at the Mannheim National Theater

1785 After six years of censorship, *The Marriage of Figaro* by Beaumarchais is presented in Paris

1790 Emperor Qianlong invites theater groups from the provinces to Beijing. Out of the combination of various music styles arises the Beijing Opera

1817 Gas lighting is introduced in the theater

1828 Goethe's *Faust I* opens in Paris

1830 Diderot publishes his *Paradox of the Actor*; premiere of Victor Hugo's *Hernani* ignites a major theater scandal. At a performance of the opera *The Silent Woman of Portici* by Auber, the Brussels audience storms the Palace of Justice after the "Freedom Duet" in the second act and begins the revolt that leads to Belgian independence

1852 Grandiose opening of *La Dame aux Camelias*, a classic of the boulevard theater, by Alexandre Dumas

1874–90 The ensemble of the Meiningen court theater tours Europe

1879 First Shakespeare festival is held in his home town of Stratford-upon-Avon; Ibsen writes *A Doll's House*

1881 Disastrous fire in the Ring Theater in Vienna; introduction of electric theater lighting

1887 Antoine founds the Théâtre Libre in Paris

1893 As a closed private association, the Free Stage evades state censorship at the premiere of Hauptmann's *The Weavers*

1895 First film showing in Paris; Oscar Wilde, *The Importance of Being Earnest*

1896 Chekhov's *The Seagull* is a flop at its St. Petersburg premiere; introduction of the revolving stage

1898 Stanislavsky founds the Moscow Art Theater

A brief overview ... Theater collections

1902 George Bernard Shaw, *Mrs. Warren's Profession*

1905 Max Reinhardt becomes head of the German Theater in Berlin

1906 Edward Gordon Craig stages Ibsen's *Rosmersholm* with Eleonora Duse in the lead in Florence

1912 The German Stage Union demands license limitations for film companies

1918 Natalia Saz founds the first children's theater with its own playhouse in Moscow

1920 Mass spectacle *The Storming of the Winter Palace* in Leningrad; opening of the first Salzburg Festival with Hofmannsthal's *Everyman*

1928 Premiere of *The Threepenny Opera* by Brecht and Weill in Berlin

1933– 4,000 German-speaking dramatists and theater professionals are forced by the Nazis into exile, among them Brecht, Reinhardt, Piscator, Zuckmayer, and Viertel

1939 Eugene O'Neill, *Long Day's Journey Into Night*

1947 Julian Beck and Judith Malina found Living Theatre Productions

1949 Brecht and Helene Weigel found the Berliner Ensemble; Elia Kazan directs the premiere of Arthur Miller's *Death of a Salesman*

1953 Samuel Beckett's *Waiting for Godot* opens in Paris

1962 Founding of the Berlin Playhouse on the Hallisch Shore, a private theater based on a democratic production and organizational model

1964 Ariane Mnouchkine establishes the collective Théâtre du Soleil in Paris

1966 Founding of the Theater for Children in the Berlin Reichskabaret, since 1972 known as the Grips Theater

1965 Peter Brook stages Peter Weiss's *The Persecution and Assassination of Marat as Performed by the Inmates of the Asylum of Charenton under the Direction of the Marquis de Sade* (known for short as *Marat/Sade*)

1967 Tom Stoppard's *Rosencrantz and Guildenstern Are Dead* launches the author's career as one of the most successful later-20th-century dramatists

1968 The Theatres Act is passed, abolishing government censorship of theater in England

1970 Peter Brook establishes the International Centre of Theatre Research in Paris

1982 *Master Harold ... And the Boys*, a drama about apartheid by South African playwright Athol Fugard opens in New York

1985 *The Mahabharata*

1993 Tony Kushner's *Angels in America: A Gay Fantasia on National Themes, Part I, Millennium Approaches* opens on Broadway; *Part II, Perestroika* opens later in the year; closing of the Schiller Theater in Berlin leads to a nationwide debate over the threatened demise of the German city theater system

Theater collections

Austria
Vienna
Österreichisches Theatermuseum
Lobkovitzplatz 2
1010 Wien
(1) 5 12 88 00-0

Denmark
Copenhagen
Teaterhistorisk Museum
Christiansborg
Ridebane 10
1218 Copenhagen
33 11 51 76

France
Paris
Bibliothèque de l'Arsénal
1, rue de Sully
75004 Paris
(1) 42 77 44 21

Theater collections

Germany
Berlin
Stiftung Archiv der Akademie
der Künste
Hanseatenweg 10
10557 Berlin
(030) 39 00 07-60

Hamburg
Zentrum für Theaterforschung
Hamburger Theatersammlung
Von-Melle-Park 3
20146 Hamburg
(040) 41 23 48-26/27

Cologne
Theaterwissenschaftliche
Sammlung
Universität zu Köln
Schloß Wahn
Burgallee 2
51127 Köln
(02203) 6 41 85

Munich
Deutsches Theatermuseum
Galeriestraße 4a
Hofgartenarkaden
80539 München
(089) 22 24 49

Great Britain
London
Theatre Museum
Russel Street
London WC2E 7PA
(171) 8 36 78 91

Victoria and Albert Museum
Cromwell Road
South Kensington
London SW7 2RL
(171) 9 38 85 00

Italy
Milan
Museo teatrale alla scala
Via Filodrammatici 2
20121 Milano
(2) 805 34 18

Rome
Biblioteca e raccolta teatrale
del Burcardo
Via del Sudario 44
00186 Roma
(6) 68 80 67 55

Japan
Tokyo
Tsubouchi Memorial Theatre
Museum
Waseda University 6-1
Nishi-Waseda1 chome
Shinjuku-ku
169 Tokyo
(3) 32 03 41 41

Netherlands
Amsterdam
Nederlands Theaterinstituut
en Theatermuseum
Herengracht 168
PB 19304
1016 BP Amsterdam
(20) 6 23 51 04

Norway
Oslo
Teatermuseet
Nedre Slottsgate 1
0157 Oslo 1
22 41 81 47

Poland
Warsaw
Muzeum Teatralne
Ul. Moliera 3/5
00950 Warszawa
(22) 26 30 01

Russia
Moscow
Theater Museum Bakhrushin
Ul. Bachrušina 31/12
113054 Moscow
(095) 2 35 37 87

St. Petersburg
Theater Museum
Ostrovskogo 6

191011 St. Petersburg
(812) 31 55 243

Sweden
Stockholm
Drottningholms Teatermuseum
Borgvägen 1-5
Box 27050
10251 Stockholm
(8) 6 65 14 00

Switzerland
Bern
Schweizerische
Theatersammlung
Schanzenstraße 15
Postfach
3001 Bern
(31) 23 52 52

United States
Cambridge, Mass.
Harvard University
32 Quincy St.
Cambridge, MA 02138
(617)495-9400

Austin, Texas
Hoblitzelle Theatre Arts
Library
University of Texas
21st & Guadalupe
Austin, TX 78705
(512)471-8944

Madison, Wisconsin
Wisconsin Center for Film
and Theatre Research
University of Wisconsin
800 University Avenue
Madison, WN 53706
(608)263-2340

New York, NY
Public Library for the
Performing Arts
40 Lincoln Center Plaza ,
New York, NY 10023-7498
(212)870-1630

Bibliography

Bibliography

Adams, Joseph Q. *Shakespearean Playhouses: A History of English Theatres from the Beginning to the Reformation.* Magnolia: Peter Smith Publications, 1959.

Allen, James T. *Greek Theatre in the Fifth Century Before Christ.* Reprint, Brooklyn: MSG Haskell House, 1969.

Artaud, Antonin. *The Theater and Its Double.* New York: Grove, 1958.

Aylen, Leo. *The Greek Theater.* Reprint, Cranbury: Fairleigh Dickinson University Press, 1973.

Baker, Barton. *History of the London Stage and Its Famous Players 1576– 1903.* Reprint, North Stratford: Ayer Company Publishers, Inc., 1972.

Baldry, H.C. *The Greek Tragic Theatre.* Reprint, New York: W.W. Norton & Company, Inc., 1973.

Banham, Martin, ed. *The Cambridge Guide to Theatre.* Cambridge: Cambridge University Press, 1995.

Beadle, Richard, ed. *The Cambridge Companion to Medieval English Theatre.* New York: Cambridge University Press, 1994.

Beauman, Sally. *The Royal Shakespeare Company: A History of Ten Decades.* New York: Oxford University Press, 1982.

Beck, Julian. *The Life of the Theatre.* San Francisco: City Lights, 1972.

Bentley, Eric. *The Life of the Drama.* New York: Atheneum, 1964.

The Playwright as Thinker: A Study of Drama in Modern Times. New York: Harcourt Brace World, 1967.

In Search of Theatre. Reprint, Tucson: BK Publications, Inc., 1991.

Berthold, Margot. *The History of World Theater: From the Beginnings to the Baroque.* New York: Frederick A. Unger Books, 1990.

Bloom, Ken. *Broadway: An Encyclopedic Guide to the History, People and Places of Times Square.* New York: Facts On File, Inc., 1990.

Blum, Daniel. *Theatre World 1944–45.* Cheshire: Biblo & Tannen Booksellers & Publishers, Inc., 1969.

—. *Theatre World 1945–46.* Cheshire: Biblo & Tannen Booksellers & Publishers, Inc., 1969.

—. *Theatre World 1946–47.* Cheshire: Biblo & Tannen Booksellers & Publishers, Inc., 1969.

Booth, Michael R. *Theatre in the Victorian Age.* New York: Cambridge University Press, 1991.

Bordman, Gerald. *The American Theatre: A Chronicle of Comedy & Drama, 1869–1914.* New York: Oxford University Press, 1994.

—. *The American Theatre: A Chronicle of Comedy &*

Drama, 1914–1930. New York: Oxford University Press, 1995.

—. *The Oxford Companion to the American Theatre.* New York: Oxford University Press, 1992.

Brandon, James R. & Martin Banham, eds. *The Cambridge Guide to Asian Theatre.* New York: Cambridge University Press, 1993.

Bratton, J.S., et al. *Acts of Supremacy: The British Empire and the Stage 1790–1903.* North Wichita: St. Martin's Press, Inc., 1991.

Brecht, Bertolt. *Brecht on Theatre: the Development of an Aesthetic.* New York: Hill and Wang, 1960.

Brecht, et al. *Essays on the German Theater.* Edited by Margaret Hertzfeld-Sander. New York: Continuum Publishing Co., 1985.

Brockett, Oscar G. *The Essential Theatre.* Orlando: Harcourt Brace College Publishers, 1992.

—. *History of the Theatre.* 7th ed. Needham Heights: Allyn & Bacon, Inc., 1994.

Brockett, Oscar and Robert R. Findlay. *Century of Innovation: A History of European and American Theatre & Drama, 1870– 1970.* 2nd ed. Allyn & Bacon, Inc., 1990.

Brook, Peter. *The Empty Space.* New York: Atheneum, 1968.

—. *The Open Door: Thoughts on Acting and Theatre.* New York: Pantheon, 1993.

Bibliography

—. *The Shifting Point: Theatre, Film, Opera, 1946–1987.* New York: Theatre Communications Group, 1987.

Brownstein, Rachel M. *Tragic Muse: Rachel of the Comédie Française.* Durham: Duke University Press, 1995.

Brustein, Robert. *Critical Moments: Reflections on Theatre and Society, 1973–1979.* New York: Random House, 1980.

Bulwer-Lytton, Edward G. *Bulwer & Macready: A Chronicle of the Early Victorian Theatre.* Edited by Charles H Shattuck. Reprint, Ann Arbor: Books on Demand.

Burton, Ernest J. *The British Theatre: Its Repertory and Practice 1100–1900 A.D.* Reprint, Westport: Greenwood Publishing Group, Inc., 1977.

Champagne, Lenora. *French Theatre Experiment Since 1968.* Ann Arbor: Books On Demand.

Coad, Oral. *American Stage.* Reprint, Tenacola: Reprint Services Corp., 1993.

Cole, Toby, ed. *Playwrights on Playwriting.* New York: Hill and Wang, 1960.

—. *Actors on Acting.* New York: Crown, 1970.

Crump, James I. *Chinese Theater in the Days of Kublai Khan.* Reprint, Ann Arbor: Books on Demand.

Deak, Frantisek. *Symbolist Theater: The Formation of an Avant-Garde.* Balti-

more: John Hopkins University Press, 1993.

Dunlap, William. *History of the American Theater.* Reprint, Tenacola: Reprint Services Corp., 1992.

Eliot, T.S. *Essays on Elizabethan Drama.* New York: Harcourt Brace World, 1956.

Engle, Ron and Tice L. Miller, eds. *The American Stage: Social and Economic Issues from the Colonial Period to the Present.* New York: Cambridge University Press, 1993.

Esslin, Martin. *Brecht: The Man and His Work.* Garden City, Anchor Books, 1961.

—. *The Encyclopedia of World Theater.* New York, Scribner, 1977.

—. *The Theatre of the Absurd,* 3rd ed. Harmondsworth, UK: Penguin, 1985.

FulopMiller, Rene & Gregor, Joseph. *Russian Theatre.* North Stratford: Ayer Company Publishers, Inc., 1972.

Gentili, Bruno. *Theatrical Performance in the Ancient World: Hellenistic and Early Roman Theatre (London studies in classical philology).* Philadelphia: John Benjamin North America, Inc.

Gilder, Rosamond. *Enter the Actress: The First Women in Theatre.* New York: Routledge, Chapman & Hall, Inc., 1959.

Grose, Kenworthy. *History of Western Theatre: A Mirror to Life.* Orlando: Harcourt Brace College Publishers, 1985.

Grotowski, Jerzy. *Towards a Poor Theatre* (pub. by Methuen UK) Portsmouth: Heinemann, Div. of Reed Elsevier, 1991.

Guicharnaud, Jacques. *Anthology of Twentieth Century French Theater.* New York: French and European Publications, Inc., 1967.

Gurr, Andrew. *The Shakespearean Stage, 1574–1642.* Cambridge: Cambridge University Press, 1970.

Harris, Andrew B. *Broadway Theatre* (pub. by Tavistock UK) New York: Routledge, Chapman & Hall, Inc., 1994.

Harris, John W. *The Medieval Theatre in Context.* New York: Division of Routledge, Chapman & Hall, Inc., 1992.

Harrison, G.B. *Elizabethan Plays and Players.* Ann Arbor: University of Michigan Press, 1956.

Hartnoll, Phyllis. *The Theatre: A Concise History.* Rev. ed. (World of Art Ser.). New York: Thames & Hudson, 1985.

Hawkins, Frederick. *Annals of the French Stage From Its Origin to the Death of Racine.* 2 vols. reprint. Brooklyn: MSG Haskell House, 1969.

—. *Annals of the French Stage from Its Origin to the Death of Racine.* reprint. Saint Clare Shores: Scholarly Press, Inc., 1968.

—. *French Stage in the Eighteenth Century.* 2 vols. reprint. Saint Clare Shores:

Bibliography

Scholarly Press, Inc., 1968.

Hemmings, F.W. *The Theatre Industry in Nineteenth Century France*. New York: Cambridge University Press, 1993.

—. *Theatre and State in France, 1760–1905*. New York: Cambridge University Press, 1994.

Hogedoorn, Wiebo, ed. *German and Dutch Theatre, 1600–1848* (Theatre in Europe: A Documentary History Ser.). New York: Cambridge University Press, 1993.

Idemn, Wilt L. and Stephen H. West. *Chinese Theater, 1100–1450: A Source Book*. Philadelphia: Coronet Books, 1982.

Jardier, Enrique G. *Studies of Spanish Theatre*. Columbia: South Asia Books, 1993.

Kennard, Joseph S. *Italian Theatre*, 2 vols. North Stratford: Ayer Company Publishers, Inc., 1972.

Kiebuzinska, Christine. *Revolutionaries in the Theater: Meyerhold, Brecht & Witkiewicz*. Edited by Oscar Brockott. reprint. Ann Arbor: Books on Demand.

King, Bruce, ed. *Contemporary American Theatre*. Wichita: St. Martin's Press, Inc., 1991.

Klaus, Carl H., et al. *Stages of Drama: Classical to Contemporary Theater*. N. Wichita: St. Martin's Press, Inc., 1994.

Knox, Bernard. *Word & Action Essays on the Ancient Theater*. Reprint. Baltimore: John Hopkins University Press, 1986.

Kovenik, Frances M. *British Drama 1660–1779: A Critical History*. Old Tappan: MacMillan Publishing Company, 1995.

Kurtiz, Paul. *The Making of Theatre History*. Englewood Cliffs: Prentice Hall, 1987.

Lawrence, William J. *Old Theatre Days & Ways*. Reprint. (Pub. by Blom Pubns UK) North Stratford: Ayer Co. Pubs., Inc., 1972.

Leach, Robert. *Revolutionary Theatre*. New York: Div. of Routledge, Chapman & Hall, Inc., 1994.

Leiter, Samuel L. *From Stanislavsky to Barrault*. Westport: Greenwood Publishing Group, Inc., 1991.

Ley, Graham. *A Short Introduction to the Ancient Greek Theater*. Chicago: University of Chicago Press, 1991.

Londre, Felicia H. *The History of World Theater: From the English Restoration to the Present*. (F. Unger Books) New York: Continuum Publishing Co., 1991.

Luciani, Vincent. *A Concise History of the Italian Theatre*. New York: S.F. Vanni, 1961.

Mackerras, Colin, ed. *Chinese Theater: From Its Origin to the Present Day*. reprint. Honolulu: University of Hawaii Press, 1989.

Mantzius, Karl. *A History of Theatrical Art in Ancient & Modern Times*. 6 vols. Magnolia: Peter Smith Publications.

Maslon, Laurence, ed. *The Arena Adventure: The First Forty Years*. New York: Applause Theatre Book Publishers, 1990.

McKendrick, Melveena. *Theatre in Spain 1490–1700*. New York: Cambridge University Press, 1992.

Meserve, Walter J. and Mollie A. Meserve. *A Chronological Outline of World Theater*. New York: Feedback Theatrebooks & Prospero Press, 1992.

Miller, Anne I. *Independent Theatre in Europe, 1887 to the Present*. North Stratford: Ayer Company Publishers, Inc., 1972.

Mitchley, Jack and Spalding, Peter. *Five Thousand Years of the Theatre*. New York: Holmes & Meier Pubs., Inc., 1982.

Moreh, Shmuel. *Live Theatre and Dramatic Literature in the Medieval Arabic World*. New York: Columbia University Press, 1991.

Mulryne, J.R. and Margaret Shewring, eds. *Italian Renaissance Festivals and Their European Influence*. Lewiston: Edwin Mellen Press, 1992.

Munich and Theatrical Modernism: Politics, Playwriting, and Performance 1890–1914. Cambridge: Harvard University Press, 1985.

Bibliography ... Index

Munshower, Susan S. *All the World's a Stage...Art&Pagentry in the Renaissance & Baroque.* 2 pts. University Park: Pennsylvania State University Department of Art History, 1990.

Nagler, Alois M. *Sourcebook in Theatrical History.* New York: Dover Publications, Inc., 1952.

Olivier, Laurence. *Confessions of an Actor: An Autobiography.* New York: Penguin, 1984.

Orgel, Stephen. *The Illusion of Power: Political Theater in the English Renaissance.* reprint. Berkeley: University of California Press

Ortolani, Benito. *The Japanese Theatre: From Shamanistic Ritual to Contemporary Pluralism.* 1995 Princeton: Princeton University Press, 1991.

Plunka, Gene A., ed. *Antoine Artaud & the Modern Theatre.* Cranbury: Fairleigh Dickinson University Press, 1994.

Porter, Susan L. *With an Air Debonair: Musical Theatre in America 1785–1815.* Washington, D.C.: Smithsonian Institution Press, 1992.

Rehm, Rush. *Greek Tragic Theatre.* New York: Division of Routledge, Chapman & Hall, Inc., 1994.

Richards, Kenneth and Laura. *The Commedia dell'Arte: A Documentary History.* Cambridge: Subsidiary of Basil Blackwell, Ltd., 1989.

Root-Bernstein, Michele. *Boulevard Theater & Revolution in Eighteenth-Century Paris.* Reprint. Ann Arbor: Books on Demand.

Rouse, John. *Brecht and the Western German Theatre: The Practice and Politics of Interpretation.* Edited by Oscar Brockett. Reprint. Ann Arbor: Books on Demand.

Schoenbaum, S. *Shakespeare's Lives.* Oxford: Clarendon Press, 1991.

Senclick, Laurence, ed. *National Theater in Northern & Eastern Europe, 1746–1900.* New York: Cambridge University Press, 1991.

Stanislavsky, Konstantin. *Stanislavsky on the Art of the Stage.* New York: Hill and Wang, 1961.

Stenberg, Douglas G. *From Stanislavsky to Gorbachev; The Theatre Studios of Leningrad.* New York: Peter Lange Publishing, Inc., 1995.

Turnell, Martin. *Classical Moment: Studies of Corneille, Molière and Racine.* Reprint. Westport: Greenwood Publishing Group, Inc., 1971.

Tynan, Kenneth. *Curtains.* New York: Atheneum, 1961.

Varaponde, M.L. *History of Indian Theatre,* vol. 1. Columbia: South Asia Books, 1987.

Vince, Ronald W., ed. *A Companion to the Medieval Theatre.* Westport: Greenwood Publishing Group, Inc., 1989.

—. *Renaissance Theatre: A Histriographical Handbook.* Westport: Greenwood Publishing Group, Inc., 1994.

Vince, Ronald W. *Ancient & Medieval Theatre: A Historiographical Handbook.* Westport: Greenwood Publishing Group, Inc., 1984.

Watson, Jack & McKernie, Grant. *A Cultural History of the Theatre.* White Plains: Longman Publishing Group, 1993.

Wickham, Glynne W. *A History of the Theatre,* 2nd ed. New York: Cambridge University Press, 1992.

Wilson, Edwin & Goldfarb, Alvin. *Living Theater: An Introduction to Theater History.* New York: The McGrawHill Co., 1983.

—. *Living Theater: A History,* 2nd ed. New York: The McGraw Hill Co., 1994.

Subject index

Académie Française 82f., 156

Actors Studio 125

actor, lay 45, 140, 141

actor/character/performer 15, 21, 22, 23, 24, 28, 30, 36, 54, 60, 71, 85, 90, 91, 93, 98, 99, 100, 102, 103, 108, 109, 135

actress 77, 78, 79, 86, 88-93, 115

Admiral's Men, The 70

Index

aesthetic 57
agit-prop theater/group 144, 145
Agon 14ff.
Agora 14
alienation 147, 148
Angura 31
animal pantomime 28
Antiquity 13-21, 52
aragoto 31, 33
art theater 142
Attelane 20, 21
auto sacramentale 78, 80
avant-garde 132, 133, 134, 137, 140, 142, 143

Backer 160
ballet 57, 59, 62, 82, 112, 134, 139
Ballet de la nuit 82
banning of performance 73, 79, 87
Barong play 22
Baroque 60ff., 80, 81, 82, 83, 84
Beijing Opera 22, 23, 27ff.
Berlin Ensemble 148, 149
Berlin Schaubühne 158
Bharata Nātyam 24
Biomechanic 142f.
Blue Blouses 141, 142
body language 23, 98, 167
boulevard theater 112
Bread and Puppet Theater (New York) 163, 165,169
Broadway 149, 158ff.
Buen Retiro 81
Bugaku 22, 31
Burgtheater (Vienna) 106
Burlesca 80
burlesque, child-bishop 39
burlesque, donkey 39
Butô 31

Camerata Fiorentina 50
canovaccio 66, 67
Cartoucherie, Paris 157
censorship 73, 97, 99, 111, 118, 119, 120, 132, 140, 170

chamber drama 19
chorege 14, 21
choreography 14, 33, 135, 139, 161
chorus 15, 17, 21, 31, 57
cinema 128–131
cinematograph 128f.
Circus Busch 139
city theater 158
Classical Unities 55, 74, 83, 97, 104
clown play 154
CLOWNPOWER 164
co-fabulist 149
comedia de figurón 80
comedia de santos 80
comedia del teatro 80
comedia en capa y espada 80
Comédie Française (Paris) 82, 85, 91, 105, 114
Comédie Italienne (Paris) 69, 82, 86
comédie-ballet 86
Comédiens du roi 82
comedy 17ff., 53ff., 59, 69, 73ff., 87, 103, 104, 126
comedy of character 87
comedy of humors 75
comedy of manners 86
comedy of mistaken identity 19
comedy of types 86
comedy, bourgeois 99
comedy, Italian Renaissance 57
Comedy, Middle 17
Comedy, New 17, 19
Comedy, Old 17
comedy, scholastic 53f., 55
comedy, situation 87
commedia dell'arte 23, 46, 53, 64ff., 82, 86, 89, 90, 139, 142, 164
commedia erudita 53, 54, 57, 65
Compagnia dei Gelosi 90
Compagnie des Films d'Art 129

Compagnie Jérôme Deschamps 170, 171
costume 15, 18, 21, 24, 25, 29, 32, 52, 57, 62, 63, 73, 92, 114, 117, 141, 165
Court Theater (Weimar) 108
cubism 142
The Curtain (London) 70

dadaism 136
dalang 26, 27, 28
dance 9, 10, 20, 22, 24, 26, 30, 31, 32, 35, 44
dance theater 22, 23, 28, 32, 153
dance theater, Indian 22, 24, 25
dancer 9, 10, 11, 21, 36
declamation 57
decoration 25, 45, 62, 63
Deus ex machina 15
deuteragonist 15, 21
Deutsches Theater (Berlin) 122, 138
dialogue 15, 55, 69, 74
Dionysian cult 13, 17
Dionysian Theater 14
director 14, 60, 96, 100, 102, 106, 116, 124
dithyrambos 15, 21
drama, allegorical 42
drama, classic 35, 107
drama, cloak and dagger 80f.
drama, humanistic 57
drama, pastoral 55f., 69
drama, Restoration 100
drama, Sanskrit 22, 24
drama, secular 42f.
drama, Spanish 78ff.
drama, spoken 22, 28, 31
dramatic rules, classical 75, 112
dramatic theory 101, 124
dramaturgy 16, 23, 103
dramma per musica 56
Düsseldorf Playhouse 99

Index

eleas 17
Elizabethan Theater 70-74
Els Joglars 170
Enlightenment 94f., 96, 98,
    103, 104, 105, 106,
    107, 108, 111, 114
entremese 80
Epidauros, amphitheater 44
existentialism 155
Expressionism 143

farce 28, 43, 82, 86, 156,
    158
film 128-131, 132, 133,
    136, 139, 145, 148,
    158, 160, 161, 163,
    164, 170, 171
finger language 24
The Fortune (London) 70
fourth wall 49, 102, 118
Freie Bühne (Berlin) 119,
    121, 123
French Revolution 95, 108

Gentlemen's Room 72
German Bühnenverein 157
gesture 23, 129
Gigaku 22, 31
The Globe (London) 70, 71,
    75
Golden Age 60-87
Gosudarstvenny Detski
    Music Theater (Moscow)
    150
Grønnegadeteater
    (Denmark) 96
Great Dionysian Festival 13,
    14, 21
Grips Theater 151, 153

Hamburg National Theater
    103, 105
Happening 162
historicism 114, 117
Hôtel de Bourgogne (Paris)
    82, 85
humanism 51, 55, 76
Illustre Théâtre 86
Impressionism 110
improvisation/impromptu

53, 64, 65, 66, 69, 89,
    101
Independent Theatre Society,
    London 119
interlude 30, 42, 55, 57,
    59, 80
Intermedium 52, 57
itinerant troupe 65, 68, 79,
    82, 102, 156

Jacobin Terror 95, 107,
    108
jester/juggler 24, 36, 46,
    65
Jôruri 31, 32

kabuki 23, 30, 31, 32f.
Kagura 31
Kathakali 25f.
katharsis 17
Khon 23
kyogen 30, 31

law of the estates 55
lazzo 65f., 68
lighting 116, 137, 138,
    143, 148
liturgy 37f.
living newspaper 141
Living Theatre 165, 167f.
loge 72
long run 159
Lord Chamberlain's Men 69,
    70
Lucerne Easter play 40
ludi Romani 18

Mahābhārata 24, 26
mask 9, 15, 16, 19, 20, 21,
    23, 24, 27, 28, 29, 30f.,
    65ff., 89
mask, painted 25, 29, 31,
    33
masque 62
mass direction 118, 139
Meiningen, Court Theater
    115ff., 122
Meistersinger 43
Middle Ages 34-43, 45
mie 31, 33

Millowitsch-Theater
    (Cologne) 159
mimus 18, 20, 21, 88
minstrel 36
moral institution 96, 99,
    102, 150
Moscow Art Theater 119,
    124, 125, 126, 127
mosquetero 79
musical 159, 161, 162,
    164
mystery cycle 40, 58
mystery play 11, 45, 82,
    89, 138, 139

Nātyaśāstra 22, 23, 24
National Theater 103ff.
National Theatre (London)
    157
naturalism 117ff., 122, 123,
    124, 126, 127, 130,
    134
Norske Teatret (Oslo) 121
Nō play 22, 23, 30ff.
Odin Teatret (Dänemark)
    166
Off-Broadway 162
Off-Off-Broadway 162
Olympia Hall (London) 139
onnagata 33
opera 55f., 57, 60, 97, 163
opera house 44
operetta 112, 113
Orange, Roman theater 45
orchestra 15, 21, 44, 45,
    47

Palace Theater (Ludwigs-
    burg) 62
Palace Theater (New York)
    160
Palliata 21
pantomime 139
Pantomimus 21
Paradise Now 167
pedagogy, reformed 151
Petit Bourbon (Paris) 86
Phobos 16f.
Phylaken farce 18, 21
Piccolo Teatro (Milan) 156

Index

pièces bien faites 112
Piscator stage (Berlin) 145
play, Antichrist 38, 42
play, Christmas 39, 42
play, Corpus Christi 78
play, courtroom 134
play, Easter 38, 42
play, history 73f., 77, 112
play, Last Judgment 42
play, Laurentius 58
play, liturgical 89
play, merchant's 38
play, miracle 38, 42
play, morality 43
play, mystery 39f., 42, 51, 58
play, paradise 42
play, passion 39ff., 42, 45
play, prophet 38
play, religious 45
play, Shrove Tuesday (Fastnachtsspiel) 42, 43
play, spiritual 42
poeta laureatus 90
Previews 161
proletkult 141, 142
propaganda 57, 58
proskenion 15, 21, 44
protagonist 15, 21, 107
puppet theater 26, 27, 31, 32

Ramses Papyrus 12
ranking system (rank) 49
Rāmāyana 24, 26
Rasa 25
realism 117ff., 124, 125, 127, 159
realism, social 127
realism, socialist 127
Renaissance 47, 50-59, 60, 61, 68, 76, 89
repertory theaters 157, 163
Revolution, October 127, 132
Revolution, Russian 140
Revue 144f., 156
Rigveda 22
The Rose (London) 70, 71
Rote Grütze (Berlin) 152

Royal National Theater (Berlin) 100, 106, 114
Royal Shakespeare Company (London) 157, 168

Salzburg Festival 43
San Francisco Mime Troupe 164
Sarugaku 31
satyr play 14, 21
scaenae frons 45, 48
scena per angolo 62
scenery 47ff., 60, 62, 63, 70, 114, 117, 119
Schall und Rauch 138
Schillertheater (Berlin) 159
setting/stage decoration/scenery 48, 57, 120
Seven Meditations against Political Masochism 167
shadow theater/play 22, 26f., 27
shaman dance 28
Shimpa 31
Shingeti 31
shite 31
Shouwburg (Amsterdam) 96
sign language 20, 99
skene 15, 21, 44
slave farce 19
sottie 42f.
special effect 116
stage 29, 32, 33, 44, 47, 55, 60, 62, 70, 86, 96, 97, 99, 100, 102, 103, 108, 109, 147
stage design 62, 114, 116, 122, 134, 137, 144, 147, 148
stage lighting 137
stage machinery 42, 48, 62f., 166
stage perspective 63
stage, arena 49, 138
stage, booth 46
stage, corral 46
stage, illusionary 134
stage, itinerant 46, 102, 103

stage, peep show 49, 62
stage, perspectival 70
stage, revolving 138
stage, Shakespearean 46f., 49
stage, simultaneous 45, 47, 55
stage, single-setting 57, 136
stage, Terence (bathing-cell) 47, 55, 57
state playhouse 158
state scene 101
Strasbourg Latin School 58
Sturm und Drang 105ff., 111
supermarionette 136
Surrealisten 155
Swan, The (London) 70, 73
symbolism 124, 141
sympathy 100, 102, 109

Tag-Teatro (Venice) 69
teatro de corral 79
Teatro degli Uffizi (Florence) 52
Teatro di San Cassiano (Venice) 60
Teatro Farnese (Parma) 48, 62
Teatro Mediceo (Florence) 63
Teatro Olimpico (Vicenza) 47, 48
Teatro stabile 156
Telari 48, 70
theater aesthetic 96, 107, 108, 142
Theater at the Goosemarket (Hamburg) 105
theater club 119
Theater im Marienbad (Freiburg) 152
Theater October 141, 142
theater of allegory 81
theater of cruelty 166
theater of the absurd 154ff.
theater of the director 116
Theater of the Revolution (Moscow) 141

Index

theater reform 102, 103, 104, 105, 115, 165
theater school 22, 28
theater spaces 44-47
theater utopias 133f., 141
theater, bordello 28
theater, bourgeois 94-109, 134
theater, children's 150-153
theater, Chinese 28
Theater, classical French 105
theater, commercial 112
theater, court 48, 62
theater, epic 140, 145, 146, 147
theater, experimental 165, 166
theater, Far Eastern 22-33
theater, free/independent 159, 164, 165, 167, 169, 170
theater, French 82-87
theater, Indian 23, 24
theater, Jesuit 57, 58, 59
theater, musical 28, 32
theater, open-air 46, 62
theater, political 68, 133, 135, 140f., 144, 146, 149
theater, poor 165ff.
theater, popular 25, 62, 77, 78, 79, 159
theater, primitive 8f.
theater, private 156, 158, 163, 167
theater, professional 54, 61, 64, 71, 79, 89
Theater, Proletarian 144
theater, Roman 88
theater, Russian 123ff., 134, 140f.
theater, school 57, 58f.
theater, street 46, 68
Théâtre Antoine 120
Théâtre de Complicité (London) 171
Théâtre du Soleil 157
Théâtre Français 105
Théâtre Libre 120

Théâtre Royal (Paris) 68
The Theatre (London) 69
theatron 13, 14, 44
tier 63
Togata 21
tragédie classique 82, 85
tragedy 14, 15ff., 54ff., 69, 73f., 75, 83, 84, 85, 97, 100, 104, 105, 108, 109, 160
tragedy, Blood and Thunder 77
tragedy, bourgeois 96f., 102
tragedy, classical 16, 54, 96, 98, 101
tragedy, De casibus 54f.
tragedy, Greek 21
tragedy, heroic 98
tragedy, Roman 18, 19
tragedy, Restoration 100
tragedy, revenge 74, 77
tragicomedy 83
tritagonist 15, 21
Troupe royale 82

Västanå Theater 153
Veda 24
Venetian opera house (Vienna) 63
Volksbühne (Berlin) 104, 123, 145

Wandering players 36f.
Wayang bébér 28
Wayang golek 26, 27
Wayang klitik 26, 28
Wayang kulit 22, 26, 27
Wayang topeng 27
Wayang wong 26, 27
Wederzijds 152
Weimar style 108
Weimarer classic 105, 108
well-made plays 112
wing 70
writing workshop 146

Ziegfeld Follies 159

Index of names

Abbott and Costello 68
Adamov, Arthur 155
Aeschylus 15, 16, 157
    Agamemnon 16, 157
    The Choephori 16
    The Eumenids 16
    The Hiketiden 16
    The Oresteia 16
    The Persians 16
    Prometheus Bound 16
    Seven against Thebes 16
Albee, Edward 155, 159
    Who's Afraid of Virginia Woolf? 155, 159
Aleotti, Giovan Battista 62
Alfonso II, Duke of Ferrara 56
Amberger, Günter 103
Andreini, Isabella 91
Andrews, Julie 161
Antoine, André 119, 120
Appia, Adolphe 135ff.
Aretino, Pietro 54
    Orazia 54
Ariosto, Lodovico 53
    La cassaria 53
    I suppositi 53
Aristophanes 17, 58
    Lysistrata 17
Aristotle 8, 13, 17, 54
    Poetics 8, 17, 21, 54
Artaud, Antonin 164ff., 168
    Les Cenci 165
Astaire, Fred 161
Augustine 35

Bach, Johann Sebastian 61
Bacon, Francis 76
Balla, Giacomo 134
Balten, Pieter 42
Balzac, Honoré de 94
Barlach, Ernst 143
Barrie, Sir James Matthew 151
    Peter Pan 151

Index

Beaumarchais, Pierre Caron
de 99
The Marriage of Figaro
99
Beaumont, Francis 75
Beck, Julian 165, 167
Beckett, Samuel 154, 155
Endgame 155
Happy Days 155
Krapp's Last Tape 155
Waiting for Godot 154f.
Beethoven, Ludwig van 94
Béjart, Madeleine 86, 90
Beolco, Angelo, called
Ruzzante 54
Berlau, Ruth 146
Berlin, Irving 159
Bernhardt, Sarah 77, 88,
113, 159
Bettelheim, Bruno 152
Children Need Fairy Tales
152
Bharata Muni 23
Bibbiena, Bernardo Dovizi
da 53, 54
Calandria 53, 54
Bois, Curt 85
Bondy, Luc 97, 158
Brahm, Otto 120
Brahma 23
Brando, Marlon 125, 161
Brecht, Bertolt 97, 101, 127,
140, 144, 145, 146ff.,
151
*The Caucasian Chalk
Circle* 148, 149
Drums in the Night 147,
148
*The Good Woman of
Szechuan* 147, 148,
149
Happy End 149
The Life of Galileo 148
The Mother 127
*Mother Courage and Her
Children* 147, 148
*The Resistible Rise of
Arturo Ui* 148
Threepenny Opera 97,
149

Bronnen, Arnolt 143
Brook, Peter 44, 157, 165ff.
The Empty Space 44,
167
Mahābhārata 169
Brueghel, Pieter the Younger
42
Brühl, Karl Count of 116
Buontalenti, Bernardo 52,
63
Burbage, James 71
Burbage, Richard 69ff.
Burnacini, Giovanni 63
Burnacini, Ludovico Ottavio
63
Il pomo d'oro 63

Calderón de la Barca, Pedro
60, 81
Life Is a Dream 81
Callot, Jacques 64
Balli di Sfessania 64
Calmette, André, Charles-
Gustav-Antoine Le Bargy
*The Murder of the Duke of
Guise* 129, 130, 131
Camus, Albert 155
Carl Augustus, Prince 108
Catherine the Great 94
Cervantes Saavedra, Miguel
de 60, 80
Don Quixote 60, 80
Champmeslé, Marie
Desmare 90
Chaplin, Charlie 132
Charlemagne 34
Charles II, King of England
97
Charles V, Emperor 50
Charms, Daniil 171
*Out of a House Walked a
Man* 171
Chaucer, Geoffrey 34
Canterbury Tales 34
Chekhov, Anton 124ff., 126,
127
The Three Sisters 126
The Cherry Orchard 125
The Seagull 125, 126
Uncle Vanya 125, 126

Cleisthenes 8, 13
Close, Glenn 162
Collier, Jeremy 99
Columbus, Christopher 5
Condell, Henry 76
Congreve, William 99
Constantine I 8
Corinth, Lovis 139
Corneille, Pierre 83
Le Cid 83
The Liar (Le menteur)
Sertorius 83
Craig, Edward Gordon
135ff., 165
Cranach, Lucas the Elder
Cromwell, Oliver 73, 97

Dante Alighieri 34
Divine Comedy 34
de Bont, Ad 152, 153
Mirad—A Boy from Bosnia
153
Descartes, René 94
Deschamps, Jérôme 170,
171
Devrient, Eduard 100
Devrient, Ludwig 100
Diderot, Denis 98, 101,
102, 105
*Discours sur la poésie
dramatique* 102
Encyclopaedia 98
The Father of the Family
101
The Natural Son 101
Paradoxe sur le comédien
101
Diesel, Rudolf 110
Dietrich, Marlene 93
Dionysus 14, 15, 21, 44
Doré, Gustave 80
Dorfmann, Ariel 162
Death and the Maiden
162
Dreyfus, Richard 162
Dryden, John 97
du Parc, Mlle. 86
Dumesnil, Mlle. 84
Dürrenmatt, Friedrich 171
Visit of the Old Lady 171

Index

Duse, Eleonora 89, 113, 118, 159

Eberle, O. 9
Edwards, Jango 164
Einstein, Albert 132
Elizabeth I, Queen of England 70, 73
Engel, Johann Jacob 98
Epicurus 13
Ercole I d'Este, Duke of Ferrara 52
Euripides 16, 17, 58
  Alcestis 17
  The Bacchae 17
  Electra 16, 17
  Iphigenia in Taurus 17
  Medea 17, 20
  Oedipus Rex 16
  The Trojan Women 16, 17

Fleisser, Marieluise 146
  Der Tiefseefisch 146
Fletcher, John 75
Flickenschildt, Elisabeth 109
Fo, Dario 156
Franz Joseph II, Emperor 106
Franz, Ellen 115
Friedrich II, King of Prussia 95
Friedrich III, King of Prussia 106
Fuchs, Georg 135

Galilei, Galileo 50
Galli-Bibbiena, Fernando 62
Garrick, David 99
Gay, John 97
Genet, Jean 155
George II, Duke of Meiningen 115, 116, 117
Gershwin, George 159
Goethe, Johann Wolfgang von 98, 100, 107, 108, 109, 116
  Egmont 109
  Faust 108, 109
  Götz von Berlichingen 109

Iphigenie 109
The Sufferings of Young Werther 109
Goetz, Joseph Franz von 99
Gogol, Nikolai 142
  Revisor 142
Goldoni, Carlo 69
  The Servant of Two Masters 69
Goll, Ivan 136
  Methusela 136
Gorky, Maksim 124ff.
  The Lower Depths 124, 127
  Mother 127
  Summer Folk 127
  Vassa Zheleznowa 127
Gottsched, Johann Christoph 90, 94, 102ff.
  The Dying Cato 104
Goya, Francisco de 94
Gozzi, Carlo 69, 141
  Princess Turandot 141
Grabbe, Christian Dietrich 117
  Don Juan and Faust 117
Greene, Robert 74, 76
  Pandosto 76
Grosz, George 136
Grotowski, Jerzy 165, 166, 168
Gründgens, Gustaf 109
Guarini, Giovanni Battista 56
  Il Pastor Fido 56
Guillaume de Laris 34
  Roman de la Rose 34
Gutenberg, Johannes 50

Hackman, Gene 162
Hahn, Otto 132
Hamlisch, Marvin 163
  A Chorus Line 163
Händel, Georg Friedrich 61
Hardy, Oliver 68
Hasenclever, Walter 143
  The Son 143
Hauptmann, Elisabeth 146
Hauptmann, Gerhart 119, 120, 122f.

Before Dawn 122
Hanneles Himmelfahrt 123
The Weavers 119, 123
Haydn, Joseph 94
Heinrich, called "Frauenlob" 36
Hellman, Lillian 160
Hemminge, John 76
Henry IV, Emperor 34
Henry VIII, King of England 50
Henslowe, Philip 73
Herder, Johann Gottfried 106
Herod 41
Herodotus 8, 12
Heywood, Thomas 73
  A Woman Killed With Kindness 73
Hindemith, Paul 135
  Murder, the Women's Hope 135
Hitler, Adolf 132, 148
Hobbes, Thomas 60, 94
  Leviathan 60
Hofmannsthal, Hugo von 43
  Jedermann 43
Hogarth, William 79
Holberg, Ludvig 96
  Jeppe from Berge 96
Holinshed, Raphael 77
  Chronicles of England, Scotland and Ireland 77
Homer 8
  Iliad 8
  Odyssey 8
Hugo, Victor 112, 114
  Hernani 112
  Lucrèce Borgia 114
Hume, David 94, 95

Ibsen, Henrik 118, 120ff.
  A Doll's House 120, 121, 122, 123
  An Enemy of the People 122
  Ghosts 120, 122, 123
  Hedda Gabler 120

Index

The Pillars of the Community 120
Rosmersholm 89, 118
The Wild Duck 122
I-Cher-Nofret 11
Iffland, August Wilhelm 100
Ionesco, Eugène 155, 156
   The Bald Soprano 156
   The Chairs 155
   Rhinoceros 156

Jarry, Alfred 137
   Ubu Roi 137
Jevreinov, Nikolai Nikolaievich 141
   The Storming of the Winter Palace 141, 142
Jhering, Herbert 145
John, King of England 77
Jones, Inigo 62
Jonson, Ben 62, 74, 75, 77
   Bartholomew Fair 75
   Volpone 75
Jürgens, Curd 43

Kainz, Josef 114
Kaiser, Georg 143
Kalidasa 25
   Sakuntala 25
Kaname 30
Kant, Immanuel 94, 95
Kaulbach, Wilhelm von 116
Kean, Charles 114, 115, 116
Kean, Edmund 76, 114, 159
Kleist, Heinrich von 108, 115, 117
   Amphytrion 109
   The Broken Jug 109
   Hermannsschlacht 117
   Penthesilea 109
   Prince of Homburg 109
Klinger, Friedrich M. 107
   The Twins 107
Koch, Robert 110
Kokoschka, Oskar 135
Kollwitz, Käthe 119
Korn, Benjamin 103
Kruse, Max 139

Kushner, Tony 162
   Angels in America 162
Kusmardjo, Subroto 26
Kyd, Thomas 74, 75
   Hamlet 74
   The Spanish Tragedy 74

Lafitte brothers 129
Lang, Fritz 131
   Metropolis 131
Lao-Tse 22
Laurel, Stan 68
Lecoq, Jacques 171
Lenz, Jakob Michael Reinhold 106
   Remarks on the Theater 106
   The Caretaker 106
Leonardo da Vinci 50, 51
Lepage, Robert 170
Lessing, Gotthold Ephraim 94, 97, 103ff., 108, 150
   Emilia Galotti 104, 105
   Hamburg Dramaturgy 105
   The Jews 105
   Minna von Barnhelm 104, 106
   Miss Sara Sampson 105
   Nathan the Wise 103
   The Young Scholar 104
Lichtenberg, Georg Christoph 98
Lillo, George 100, 105
   The London Merchant 100
Livius Andronicus 18
Li Xingdao 28
   Chalk Circle 28
Lloyd Webber, Andrew 161
Locke, John 94
Lope de Rueda 79
Lothar, Susanne 103
Louis XIII, King of France 63
Louis XIV, King of France 61, 62, 82, 86, 105
Luce, Claire 161
Ludwig, Volker 151, 153
Lumière, Auguste and Louis 110, 128

Closing Time at a Factory 128
Lunacharsky, Anatoly 140
Luther, Martin 50, 58, 59
   Table Talk 59

Machiavelli, Niccoló 53
   The Prince 53
   Mandragola 53
Malina, Judith 167
Marivaux, Pierre Carlet de Chamblain de 97
   The Triumph of Love 97
Marlowe, Christopher 75, 76, 77, 166
   Tamburlaine 75
Marx, Karl 110
   The Communist Manifesto 110
McBurney, Simon 170, 171
Méliès, Georges 110, 128, 133
   The Rubber Head 128, 133
Menander 17
Méténier 120
   En famille 120
Meyerhold, Vsevolod Emilievich 141, 142
Michelangelo 50
Miller, Arthur 160
   The Crucible 160
   Death of a Salesman 160
   A View from the Bridge 160
Millowitsch, Peter 159
Millowitsch, Willy 159
Milton, John 61
   Paradise Lost 61
Minnelli, Liza 161
Mnouchkine, Ariane 78, 157
Molière 68, 69, 85ff., 90, 115
   The Doctor in Love 86
   Don Juan 87
   The Imaginary Invalid 85, 86, 87
   The Miser 87
   The Misanthrope 87

Les Précieuses Ridicules 87
Tartuffe 87
The Tricks of Scapin 85
Molina, Tirso de 81
Monroe, Marilyn 125
Montesquieu, Charles de 94
Monteverdi, Claudio 50, 57
  Orfeo 50, 57
Moritz, Frank 149
Mozart, Wolfgang Amadeus 94
  The Magic Flute 115
Müller, Traugott 144
Munch, Edvard 122, 139

Napoleon Bonaparte 94, 110
Neher, Carola 145
Nero 8
Neuber, Friederike Caroline 90, 102, 103, 104
Neuber, Johann 90
Newman, Paul 125
Nielsen, Asta 77, 130

Odets, Clifford 160
Offenbach, Jacques 112, 113
Olivier, Sir Laurence 157
O'Neill, Eugene 159
O'Neill, James 160
  Long Day's Journey into Night 160
  The Emperor Jones 160
Opitz, Martin 60
  Book of German Poetry 60
Orlik, Emil 138
Otani Oniji 32

Palladio, Andrea 47
Peisistratos 13
Pepusch, Johann Christian 97
, *The Beggar's Opera* 97
Pericles 17
Peshkov, Aleksey Maksimo-
  vich see Gorky, Maksim
Peymann, Claus 87

Picasso, Pablo 132, 170
Pinter, Harold 155
  The Birthday Party 155
  The Caretaker 155
  The Homecoming 155
Pirandello, Luigi 139
  Six Characters in Search of an Author 139
Piscator, Erwin 140, 144ff., 148
  Red Revue 144
  Nevertheless 144, 145
Plato 8, 13
Plautus 19, 52, 53, 58, 76
  Cistellaria 19
  Menaechmi 52, 76
Poquelin, Jean-Baptiste see Molière
Porter, Cole 159
Protagoras 13
Pushkin, Alexander Sergeivich 125
  The Miserly Knight 125

Racine, Jean Baptiste 83, 84f., 86
  Alexander the Great 85
  Andromaque 84
  Bayazet 84
  Bérénice 84
  Britannicus 84
  Iphigénie 84
  The Litigants 84
  Mithridate 84
  Phèdre (Phaedra) 84
Rasser, Johann 59
  Play of Child Raising 59
Reigbert, Otto 143, 147
Reinhardt, Max 122, 138ff., 143
  Miracle 138, 139
Richelieu, Armand-Jean du Plessis de 63, 83
Rigg, Diana 168
Rooney, Mickey 139
Rousseau, Jean-Jacques 94
Rowlandson, Thomas 97
Rühmann, Heinz 154
Rushdie, Salman 154
Ruzzante s. Beolco, Angelo

Sachs, Hans 43
Samarovski, Branco 87
Sand, Maurice 66
Sandrock, Adele 77, 92
Sartre, Jean-Paul 154, 155
  The Flies 154
  No Exit 154
  Dirty Hands 154
Saz, Natalia 150
Schiller, Friedrich von 100, 106, 107, 109, 117, 144
  Bride of Messina 108
  Maid of Orleans 117
  The Robbers 100, 107, 144, 145
  Wallenstein 108, 116
  William Tell 108
Schinkel, Karl F. 114, 115
Schlemmer, Oskar 135
Schröder, Ernst 154
Schuch, Franz 101
Scofield, Paul 168
Seneca 19, 52, 54, 77
Serlio, Sebastiano 63
Shakespeare, William 60, 70, 71, 75ff., 98, 100, 105, 106, 109, 112, 113, 114, 115, 116, 129, 166, 168
  Antony and Cleopatra 98
  As You Like It 77
  Comedy of Errors 76
  Hamlet 74, 77, 98
  Henry IV 78
  Henry V 115
  Henry VIII 77, 136
  Julius Caesar 116
  King John 77
  King Lear 77, 78, 157, 168
  Macbeth 77
  The Merchant of Venice 115
  A Midsummer Night's Dream 77, 114, 139
  Titus Andronicus 74, 77
  The Winter's Tale 76, 171
Shaw, George Bernard 120, 127, 140

Index

Candida 127
*The Houses of Mr.
    Satorius* 120
Major Barbara 127
Mrs. Warren's Profession
    120, 127
Pygmalion 127
Saint Joan 127
Simon, Neil 161
Socrates 8, 13
Sophocles 15, 16, 17, 58
    Ajax 17
    Antigone 17
    Electra 17
    Oedipus Tyrannus 17
    Philoctetes 17
    The Women of Trachis 17
Spinoza, Baruch de 94
Stalin 127, 132
Stanislavsky, Konstantin
    123ff., 140
    The Work of the Actor
    124
Steffin, Margarete 146
Stein, Peter 158
Strasberg, Lee 125
Strauss, Botho 158
    Kalldewey 158
Stravinsky, Igor 134
    Fuoco d'artificio 134
Strehler, Giorgio 69, 156
Strindberg, August 120,
    121, 122
    Miss Julie 121

Tairov, Aleksander
    Yakovlevich 142
    The Unchained Theater
    142
Tandy, Jessica 161

Tasso, Torquato 56
    Aminta 56
Terayama, Shuji 165
Terence 19, 20, 47, 52,
    53, 55, 57, 58
    Adelphoe 20
Terry, Ellen 77, 135
Theodora, Byzantine Empress
    88
Tieck, Ludwig 94
Tischbein, Johann H. W. 109
Toller, Ernst 143, 146
    Hurray! We're Alive 146
    The Transformation 143
Tolstoy, Leo 120, 124
    Tsar Fodor 124
Tourneur, Cyril 74, 75
    Revenger's Tragedy
    74
Tsi-tsung, Chinese emperor
    22

Vakhtangov, Yevgeny 141
Vega, Lope de 80, 81
    *The New Art of Writing
    Plays* 80
    The Burning Village 81
Verdi, Giuseppe 110
    Aida 110
Virgil 56
Vitruvius Pollio 47, 50
    Ten Books of Architecture
    50
Voltaire, born François-Marie
    Arouet 94, 95

Waechter, Friedrich K. 150,
    152
    *The Devil with the Three
    Golden Hairs* 152

Wagner, Heinrich L. 106
    The Child Murderer 108
Wagner, Richard 110
Washington, George 94
Watt, James 94
Webber, Andrew Lloyd 162
    Cats 162, 163
    Phantom of the Opera
    163
Webster, John 75
Weigel, Helene 147
Weill, Kurt 149
Weissenborn, Friederike
    Caroline see Neuber,
    Friederike Caroline
Wiene, Robert 131
    *The Cabinet of Dr.
    Caligari* 131
Wilde, Oscar 127
    *The Importance of Being
    Earnest* 127
Wilder, Thornton 160
    Our Town 160
    The Skin of Our Teeth
    160
Williams, Tennessee 160,
    161
    Cat on the Hot Tin Roof
    160
    The Glass Menagerie
    160
    A Streetcar Named Desire
    160, 161
Wright brothers 132
Wycherley, William 100

Xuangzong, Chinese
    emperor 22, 28

Zola, Emile 121

Picture credits

Abisag Tüllmann, Frankfurt 149 c

Adel, Tomas 169 t.

Ägyptisches Museum, Turin 11 b.

Akademie der Künste, Friedrich Wolf-Archiv, Berlin 143 b.

Akademie der Künste, Theatersammlung, Berlin 144 t.

Alejnik, L, Warschau 166 t.l.

Archiv für Kunst und Geschichte, Berlin 95 b., 105 t.

Archiv Mondadori, Mailand 9, 10 t., 71 b.

Association ›Les Amis de Georges Méliès‹, Paris 128 t.

Austria, Maria, Warschau 166 b.

Badische Landesbibliothek Karlsruhe, Hs Don. 137, 138 39 b.

Balla, Luce, Rom 134 b.

Bayerische Staatsbibliothek, München 38 t., 39 t.

Bayerisches Landesamt für Denkmalpflege, München 38 M., 38 b.

Becker, Franziska, Köln Vignette 150-153

Bernbach, Lore 99 t.

Biblioteca Apostolica Vaticana 34

Bibliothek der Humboldt-Universität, Berlin 102 c. r.

Bibliothek der Rijksuniversiteit, Utrecht 73 t.

Bibliothèque de l'Arsenal, Paris 136 b. r.

Bibliothèque de l'Institut, Paris 82 t.

Bibliothèque Nationale, Paris 15 c., 35 b.

Bibliothèque-Musée de la Comédie Française, Paris 68 b., 85 t., 86 t.

Bildarchiv der Staatlichen Museen zu Berlin 115 t.

British Library, London 75 b.

British Museum, London 18 c., 72 t., 77 b.

British Travel Association 72 b.

Camera Press, London 154 b.

Centre Français-Suèdois 155 b. l.

Chinese Academy, Institute of Music and Drama, Peking 28 b.

Clausen, Rosemarie 85 b., 109 b.

Corpus Christi College, Cambridge 75 t.

Deutsche Staatsbibliothek, Berlin 103 t., 102 b. 103 c., 115 c.

Deutsches Theatermuseum, München 96 t., 113 b., 117 b., 147

Diözesanmuseum, Freising 37

Dulwich Picture Gallery/Bridgeman Art Library, London 71 t.

Eichhorn, Thomas 87 b.

English, Don 93 b.

Erwin-Piscator-Center, Archiv d. Akademie der Künste, Berlin 145 c.

Fatzer, Hans J., Hannover 152 t.

Folliot, Françoise, Paris 83 b., 84 b.

Franz, Uli, Köln 29 t.r.

From the RSC Collection with the permission of the Governors of the Royal Shakespeare Theatre, Stratford-upon-Avon 76 t.

Gaehme, Tita, Köln 78 b.

Galleria dell'Accademia, Venedig 51 t.

Galli, Max, Vogtsburg 152 b.

Gamper, Werner, Zürich 28 t.

George Altman Collection 117 t.

Goethe-Museum, Düsseldorf 108 c.

Greene, Wayne 163 b.

Grohs, Uli, Köln 159 b.

Hamburger Museum für Völkerkunde 29 t. l.

Hamburger Theatersammlung 14 b., 18, 21, 40 b., 54 c., 57 b., 56 b., 58 t., 74, 79 t., 79 c.

Kapitelbibliothek, Prag 35 t.

Kapitolinisches Musem, Rom 19 t.

Klinger, Michael, München 67 b., 164 b.

Kunstsammlungen Weimar 104 t.

Lalance, R., Paris 114 c.

Leims, Thomas, Bonn 30 t., 33, 93 t.

Maison de Victor Hugo, Ville de Paris 112 b.

Marcus, Joan 162 t.

Märkisches Museum, Berlin 106 b., 111 c., 116 t., 119 b., 138 t., 139 t., 145 b.

Mella, Federico A., Mailand 68 t.

Metropolitan Museum of Art, New York 15 b.

Michael Macintyre 10 c., 22, 23 t., 23 b., 24 b., 25 t., 26 t.

Münchner Stadtmuseum 36 c.

Musée Carnavalet, Paris 62 b., 85 t.l.

Musée des Arts Décoratifs, Paris 63

Musée du Louvre, Paris 98 t.

Musée du Vieu Biterrois, Beziers 65 t.

Museo nazionale, Neapel 14 t., 16 t., 19 b.

Museo Uffizio, Florenz 56 t.

Museum für Hamburgische Geschichte, Hamburg 105 c.

Museum of Modern Art, Film Stills Archive, New York 128 b.

Museum of the City of New York 161 c. l.

National Film and Television Archive London 133 b.

National Gallery of Scotland, Edinburgh (Privatbesitz) 95 t.

National Portrait Gallery, London 70, 75 c.

Nationalmuseum Neu Delhi 25 b.

Nationalmuseum Tokio (Kodansha) 32 t.

Öffentliche Kunstsammlung Basel, Martin Bühler 51 b., 122 t.

Olsson, Brita, S–Johanneshov 153

Österreichische Nationalbibliothek, Wien 100 b., 109 c.r., 142 c.

– Bildarchiv der Komödien des Terenz 55

Palazzo Goldoni, Venedig 69 t.

Palazzo Pitti, Florenz 54 b.

Peitsch, Peter 103 b., 149 t. r.

Photographic Technique Ltd. London 134 t.

Press Information Bureau, Giront of India, New Delhi 30 b.

Prestel Verlag München 60/61

Privatbesitz, Berlin 138 c.

Privatbesitz, Kiel 143 t.

Raccolta Teatrale Burcardo, Rom 66 t.r., 67 t.l., 113 c.

Radio Times Hulton Picture Library, London 133 t.

Rheinisches Bildarchiv, Köln 110, 158 t.

Roland-Beeneken, Frank, Berlin 151

Sabinson, Mara, San Francisco Mime Troupe 164 t.

Schmidt-Glassner, Helga, Stuttgart 62 t.

Science Museum London 132

Service Historique, Vincennes 50

Spitzing, Günter, Hamburg 26 b.

Staatliche Museen zu Berlin, Ägyptische Abteilung 11 t.

Städtische Galerie im Lenbachhaus, München 146 t.

Sulzer, Martin 12 c.

Tag Teatro, Venedig (Pressefoto) 69 t.

Teatro Olimpico, Vicenza 48

Theatermuseum Bakhrusin, Moskau 124 t., 126 b., 127 b., 141 t., 141 b.

Theaterwissenschaftliche Sammlung der Universität zu Köln 64 b. 17 t., 56 c., 88, 89, 90, 99 b., 100 t., 116 b., 136 t., 144 b., 145 t., 146 b., 148 b.

Theatre Museum, London 77 t.

Trustees of the National Gallery, London 53 t.

Uhlig, Bernd, Berlin 166 t. r., 167 c., 170

Ullmann, Gerhard, München 131 t.

Ullstein Bilderdienst 16 b.l., 92 b.

Universitätsbibliothek Heidelberg 36 t.

Victoria & Albert Museum, London 76 b., 136 b. l., 138 b.

Walz, Ruth 97 b., 158 b.

Wandel, Elke, APA Publications (HK) Ltd., Singapur 29 b.

Weihs, Angie 167 b.

Yale University Art Gallery, New Haven 94

© Nachlaß Oskar Schlemmer, I–Oggebbio 135

© VG Bild-Kunst, Bonn 1995 119 t.